THE CHILDREN'S
SPACE ATLAS

THE CHILDREN'S
SPACE ATLAS

**TAKES CHILDREN ON A VOYAGE OF
DISCOVERY FROM THE CREATION OF THE
STARS AND PLANETS TO THE LATEST
FINDINGS FROM PROBES AND SATELLITES**

ROBIN KERROD

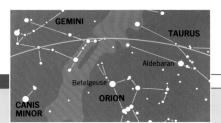

APPLE

A QUARTO BOOK

Published by The Apple Press
6 Blundell Street
London N7 9BH

ISBN 1-85076-356-9

Reprinted in 1996

This book was designed and produced by
Quarto Publishing plc
6 Blundell Street
London N7 9BH

Publishing Director Janet Slingsby
Art Director Nick Buzzard
Designer Steve Page
Illustrations Janos Marffy
Diagrams Guy Smith, David Kemp
Star Charts John Cox
Picture Manager Sarah Risley
Picture Researcher Liz Eddison

The Publishers would like to thank the following for
their help in the preparation of this book:
Bob Burns, Neal Cobourne, Penny Dawes, Stefanie
Foster, Louise Morley, Constance Novis.

Typeset in Great Britain by Bookworm Typesetting,
Manchester.
Manufactured in Singapore by Eray Scan (Pte) Ltd.
Printed in Singapore by Star Standard Industries
(Pte) Ltd.

CONTENTS

The Earth, the Moon, the Sun, the planets and the stars are bits of matter in a Universe that consists almost entirely of empty space. No one knows where the Universe begins, or where it ends. Many scientists believe it is constantly expanding and goes on for ever and ever.

EARTH AND SPACE

To us, the Earth we live on is the most important thing there is. The plants that grow on it give us food; the air around it gives us oxygen to breathe. We need both to stay alive. The Sun, far away in space, is also very important because it sends us warmth and light to brighten the sky by day.

As the Sun goes down, the sky becomes dark and night falls. When we look at the night sky – the heavens – we are peering into the inky blackness of space, across distances we cannot imagine. The stars we see look like tiny points of light. But if we could get close to them we would find that they are fiery hot suns like our Sun. They appear tiny only because they are so very far away.

On many nights the Moon appears in the sky to lighten the darkness. It looks about the same size as the Sun, but it is in fact hundreds of times smaller. It looks big only because it is hundreds of times closer to us than the Sun. Indeed, the Moon is the Earth's nearest neighbour in space.

Even though it is a neighbour, the Moon still lies a long way away by Earth standards. If we could travel to the Moon by jumbo jet, it would take us at least seventeen days. And this is only a tiny step in space. A jet trip to even the nearest star, Proxima Centauri, would take several million years!

This series of pictures shows the kinds of views of Earth we would see if we took a trip to the Moon.

Below A picture taken from the ground in Washington DC, looking at the famous Washington Monument. It stands 169 m high.

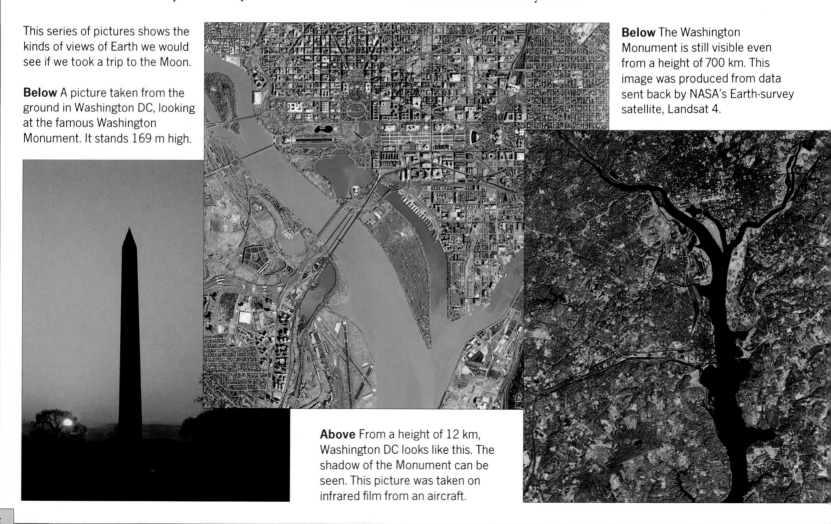

Below The Washington Monument is still visible even from a height of 700 km. This image was produced from data sent back by NASA's Earth-survey satellite, Landsat 4.

Above From a height of 12 km, Washington DC looks like this. The shadow of the Monument can be seen. This picture was taken on infrared film from an aircraft.

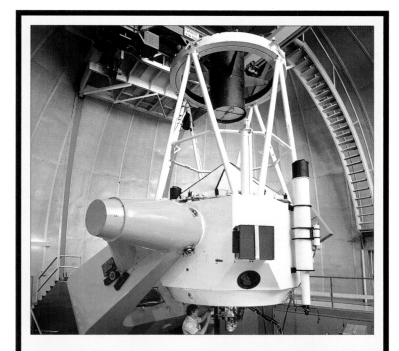

Studying space

We can study space and the bodies within it just by looking at the night sky with our eyes. But we need the help of telescopes to see the heavens in all their splendour. The telescope in the picture is used at Kitt Peak National Observatory in Arizona, USA. It has a mirror 2.1 m across, to gather the light from the stars.

Day and night

Like all large bodies in space, the Earth spins on its axis – an imaginary line running through the North and South Poles. It takes 24 hours, or one day, to spin round once. It is this spinning that brings about day and night.

It is day in the part of the Earth that is bathed in sunlight. It is night in the part of the Earth that has spun out of the light, into darkness.

We do not notice that the Earth is spinning, of course. It appears to us that the Earth stays still and that the Sun moves around it.

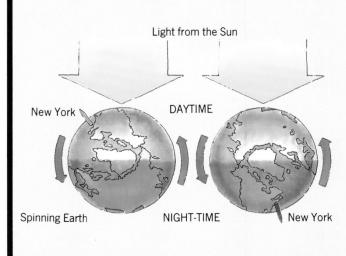

Light from the Sun

New York   DAYTIME

Spinning Earth   NIGHT-TIME   New York

Below We are now in orbit around the Moon. The Earth, some 385,000 km away, is rising above the horizon. How colourful it seems compared with the drab surface of the Moon 100 km below. This is another Apollo picture.

Above As we leave Earth, our planet stands out against the inky blackness of space. The picture, taken by Apollo astronauts, shows much of the USA clear, but there is cloud over Washington.

THE BOUNDLESS UNIVERSE

On a cloudless, moonless night, the night skies present a glorious, indeed breathtaking spectacle. It is no wonder that they have fascinated and awed people from the earliest times. The study of space and the objects in it is the science we call astronomy.

Early astronomers were skilled observers of the night sky. They mapped the positions of the stars; followed the peculiar motions of the planets; and recorded the sudden appearance of comets and 'new' stars. They also tried to explain what they saw, and put forward ideas about what the Universe — space and the bodies within it — was like.

But only in this century have astronomers really begun to understand how the Universe is made up and how enormous it is. People once thought that the Earth was the centre of the Universe, and that the stars and all the other objects circled around it. Nothing could be further from the truth.

The Earth is but a tiny speck floating in space. The illustration shows how this tiny speck fits into the rest of the Universe. The Earth is a planet, which circles with other planets around the Sun. The Sun and planets make up the Solar System. The Solar System is part of a vast Catherine wheel of stars that make up our Galaxy. In turn, our Galaxy is part of a cluster of other galaxies. Many clusters make up the Universe.

Mostly, however, the Universe consists of empty space. No one knows how big it is. Probably it just goes on for ever and ever.

The Universe is bigger than we can ever imagine. Even if we could travel at the speed of light, it would take us thousands of millions of years to travel to the most distant objects astronomers can see in their telescopes.

These pictures give an idea of how the planet we live on fits into the vast Universe. The Earth forms part of the Solar System, which is part of our Galaxy, which in turn is one of many other galaxies.

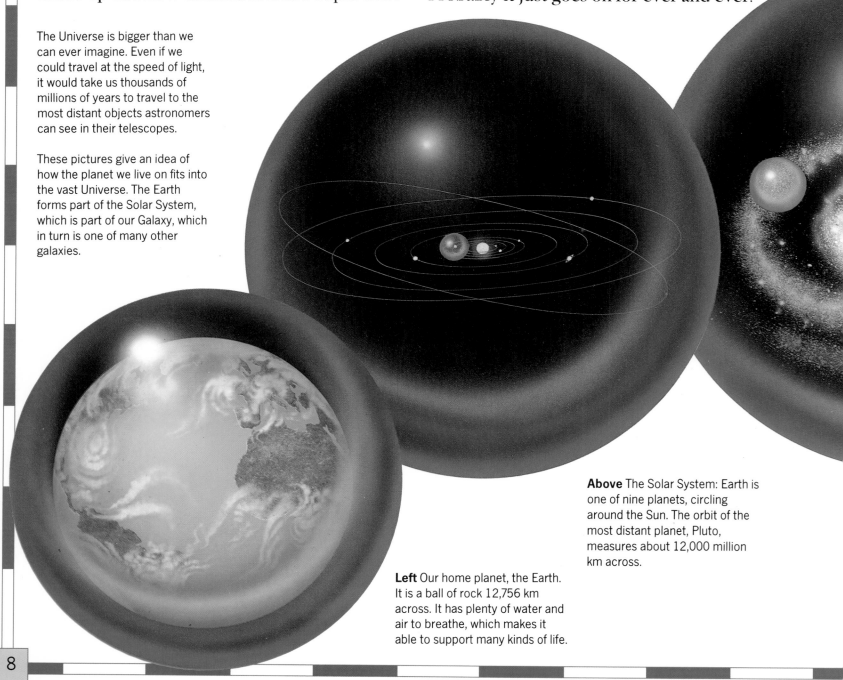

Above The Solar System: Earth is one of nine planets, circling around the Sun. The orbit of the most distant planet, Pluto, measures about 12,000 million km across.

Left Our home planet, the Earth. It is a ball of rock 12,756 km across. It has plenty of water and air to breathe, which makes it able to support many kinds of life.

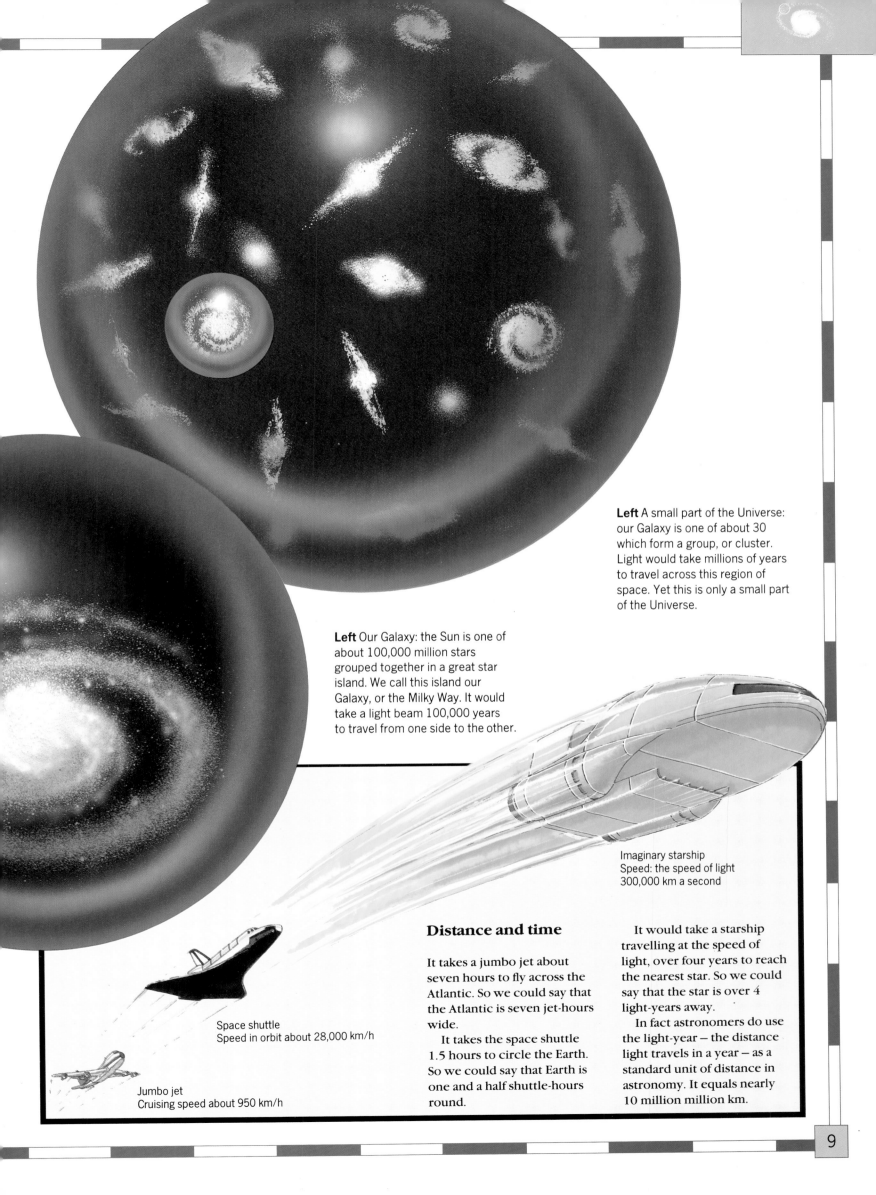

Left A small part of the Universe: our Galaxy is one of about 30 which form a group, or cluster. Light would take millions of years to travel across this region of space. Yet this is only a small part of the Universe.

Left Our Galaxy: the Sun is one of about 100,000 million stars grouped together in a great star island. We call this island our Galaxy, or the Milky Way. It would take a light beam 100,000 years to travel from one side to the other.

Imaginary starship
Speed: the speed of light
300,000 km a second

Space shuttle
Speed in orbit about 28,000 km/h

Jumbo jet
Cruising speed about 950 km/h

Distance and time

It takes a jumbo jet about seven hours to fly across the Atlantic. So we could say that the Atlantic is seven jet-hours wide.

It takes the space shuttle 1.5 hours to circle the Earth. So we could say that Earth is one and a half shuttle-hours round.

It would take a starship travelling at the speed of light, over four years to reach the nearest star. So we could say that the star is over 4 light-years away.

In fact astronomers do use the light-year – the distance light travels in a year – as a standard unit of distance in astronomy. It equals nearly 10 million million km.

SECTION 2: THE SOLAR SYSTEM

The Sun dominates our corner of the Universe. As it hurtles through space, it carries along with it a family of other bodies: planets and moons, asteroids and comets. Of the nine planets, the inner ones are relatively small and solid; the outer giants mainly consist of frozen gas.

THE SUN'S FAMILY

The Earth we live on belongs to a family that travels together through space. This is the family of the Sun, or the Solar System. The Earth is one of nine large bodies that circle around the Sun in space. These bodies are called the planets. In turn, smaller bodies circle around many of the planets. We call them satellites, or moons.

The planets circle the Sun at different speeds and at different distances from it. The planet closest to the Sun is Mercury. Then, in order of distance, come Venus, Earth, Mars, Jupiter, Saturn, Uranus, Neptune and Pluto.

Mercury, Venus, Earth and Mars lie quite close to the Sun, and are often called the inner planets. The other planets lie very much farther away from the Sun, and are called the outer planets.

The inner planets are all quite small and are made up of rock, like the Earth is. But most of the outer planets are huge and are made up mainly of gas. The inner planets have only three moons between them, but the outer ones have more than 60!

Below If we could look at the Solar System from a distance, this is what we would see. The large bodies we know as the planets travel in roughly circular paths, or orbits, around the Sun. Most of them travel in more or less the same plane (at the same level). The exception is Pluto, whose orbit takes it above and below the plane. Between the orbits of Mars and Jupiter, there is a ring of smaller bodies. These are the minor planets, or asteroids.

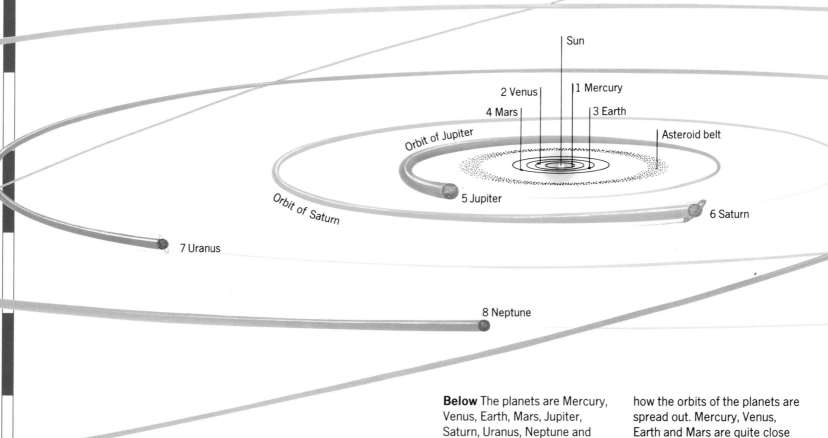

Below The planets are Mercury, Venus, Earth, Mars, Jupiter, Saturn, Uranus, Neptune and Pluto, in order of their distance from the Sun. This picture shows how the orbits of the planets are spread out. Mercury, Venus, Earth and Mars are quite close together. The others are farther apart.

Birth of the Solar System

The Sun and the planets were born nearly 5,000 million years ago. They formed out of a huge cloud of gas and dust (1).

Something caused the cloud to collapse and start to shrink under the pull of gravity. It became a spinning disc of matter with most of it lumped in the middle (2).

The middle lump got smaller and hotter. In time it began to shine as a star: it became the Sun. Other matter in the disc gradually came together to form smaller lumps of rock or gas: the planets (3).

The Solar System had become what it is today (4).

1   2   3   4

Copernicus's system

In 1453, Nicolaus Copernicus put forward the idea of a Solar System. Before then everyone thought that the Earth was the centre of the Universe. The picture shows this ancient idea.

The pull of gravity

One day in the 1660s the English scientist, Isaac Newton, was watching apples falling from a tree. It suddenly struck him that the force that pulled the apples must also pull the Moon, and this pull must keep the Moon in its orbit around the Earth. In the same way the Earth and the other planets must be kept in their orbits by the pull of the Sun.

As a result of his thoughts, Newton worked out the laws of Gravity. The basic law is that every body attracts every other body. The more mass a body has, the stronger is its gravitational pull.

The Sun, with its enormous mass, has an enormous pull, and can keep the planets in place over distances of thousands of millions of kilometres.

Orbit of Pluto

Orbit of Neptune

Orbit of Uranus

9 Pluto

Sizes of the planets

The Earth is quite a small planet. The largest planet, Jupiter, could swallow over 1,300 Earths. The picture shows the planets drawn to the same scale. Their diameters are given below.

1	Mercury	4,878 km
2	Venus	12,104 km
3	Earth	12,756 km
4	Mars	6,794 km
5	Jupiter	142,800 km
6	Saturn	120,000 km
7	Uranus	51,800 km
8	Neptune	49,500 km
9	Pluto	2,284 km

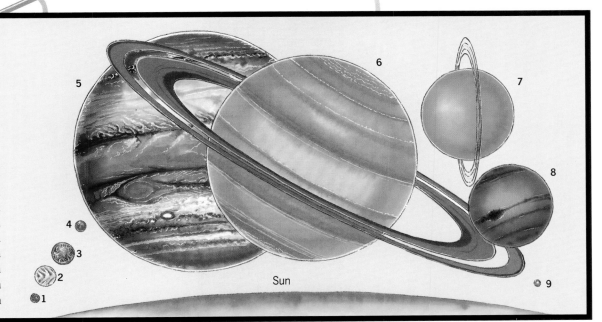

Sun

THE SUN

Every morning the Sun rises into the sky and brings light and warmth to the Earth. Without the Sun's light and heat, the Earth would be a dark, cold and lifeless planet.

The Sun is quite different from all the other bodies in the Solar System. For one thing, it is very much bigger: it could swallow more than a million Earths! For another, it is a great ball of searing hot, glowing gas. It is the only body that gives out light of its own. All the other bodies – planets, moons and comets – shine because they reflect the Sun's light.

The Sun is, in fact, a star. It is much like the other stars we see in the sky. But it appears bigger and brighter because it is so very much closer to us. If we could hitch a ride on a beam of light, it would take us only about eight minutes to reach the Sun. But it would take us four years and three months to reach the next nearest star!

Like other stars, the Sun is made up mainly of a gas called hydrogen. This gas acts like a fuel to produce the energy which keeps the Sun shining. The energy is produced deep inside the Sun. It travels slowly to the surface, from where it is given out, or radiated, as light and heat into space. We call the bright surface of the Sun, the photosphere ('light-sphere').

Above A beautiful sunset in the Caribbean. Looking like a great glowing ball, the Sun is about to sink below the horizon. Dust in the air makes the sky appear orange. Near the horizon, the Sun looks quite close, but it is in fact nearly 150 million km away.

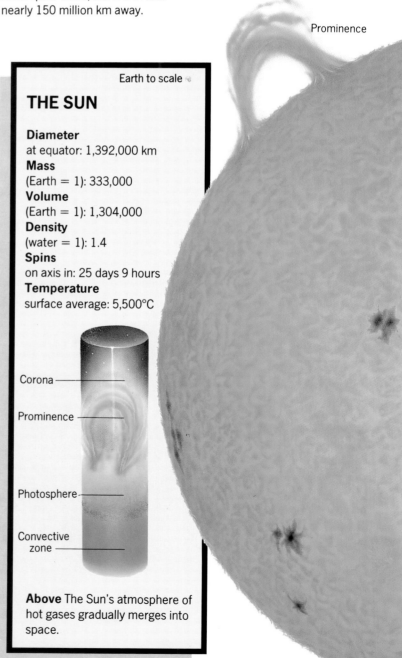

Prominence

Earth to scale

THE SUN

Diameter
at equator: 1,392,000 km
Mass
(Earth = 1): 333,000
Volume
(Earth = 1): 1,304,000
Density
(water = 1): 1.4
Spins
on axis in: 25 days 9 hours
Temperature
surface average: 5,500°C

Corona

Prominence

Photosphere

Convective zone

Above The Sun's atmosphere of hot gases gradually merges into space.

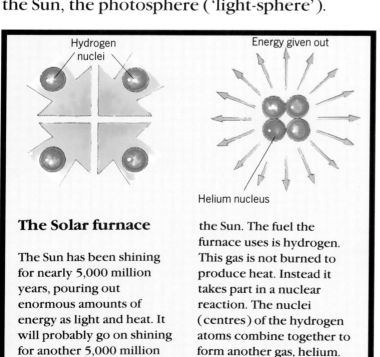

Hydrogen nuclei

Energy given out

Helium nucleus

The Solar furnace

The Sun has been shining for nearly 5,000 million years, pouring out enormous amounts of energy as light and heat. It will probably go on shining for another 5,000 million years.

This energy is produced in a 'furnace' deep inside the Sun. The fuel the furnace uses is hydrogen. This gas is not burned to produce heat. Instead it takes part in a nuclear reaction. The nuclei (centres) of the hydrogen atoms combine together to form another gas, helium. This process gives off enormous energy, which keeps the Sun shining.

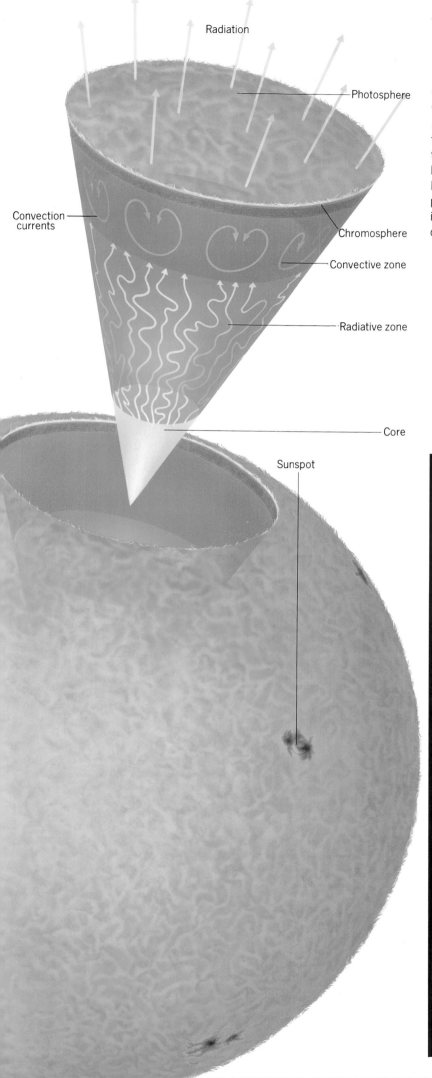

Radiation

Photosphere

Convection currents

Chromosphere

Convective zone

Radiative zone

Core

Sunspot

Left The Sun is a ball of very hot, boiling gas. The heat energy that keeps it shining is produced in a nuclear furnace in the centre, or core of the Sun. It travels away from the core as radiation, through a layer called the radiative zone. From the top of this zone, currents of gas carry the heat to the surface, through a layer called the convective zone. From the surface (called the photosphere) energy is given off into space as heat, light, and other radiation.

WARNING

Never look straight at the Sun.

The Sun is very bright, and its light can damage your eyes and even blind you.

Take special care not to look accidentally at the Sun through binoculars or a telescope.

These instruments concentrate the Sun's light and heat, making matters worse.

It is also not really safe to look at the Sun through fogged photographic film or smoked glass. These will not cut out the Sun's dangerous heat rays.

Sunshine and life

The Sun provides heat and light to the Earth, making it a place where life can exist. Sunlight is important to life because it enables plants to make their food.

Plants make their food by combining carbon dioxide (which they take in from the air) with water (which they take in from the ground). Sunlight provides the energy needed to do this. The process is called photosynthesis.

Sunshine can be harmful. If people sunbathe for too long, they get burned.

Above The ultraviolet rays in sunlight tan us, and burn us if we sunbathe too long.

Below Sunlight gives trees and other green plants the energy to make their food.

THE STORMY SURFACE

The surface of the Sun bubbles and heaves like boiling water. It has a speckled appearance, showing where little bundles, or 'cells', of gas rise and fall.

Some of the gas escapes from the surface to form an atmosphere around the Sun. The thicker, lower part of the atmosphere is called the chromosphere ('colour-sphere') because it is coloured pink. The thinner, outer part is called the corona ('crown'). From the Earth we can normally only see the pink chromosphere and pearly white corona during an eclipse, when the photosphere (the bright surface) is blotted out by the Moon (see page 30).

From time to time great fountains of gas, called prominences, erupt from the Sun's surface. They leap hundreds of thousands of kilometres into the atmosphere, often forming great loops. They take on this shape because they are held by the Sun's magnetism, or magnetic field, which acts in curved lines.

The Sun's magnetism also causes dark spots to appear on the surface. These sunspots are regions where the surface is much cooler. Around some sunspots violent eruptions called flares may occur. They send out streams of particles into space.

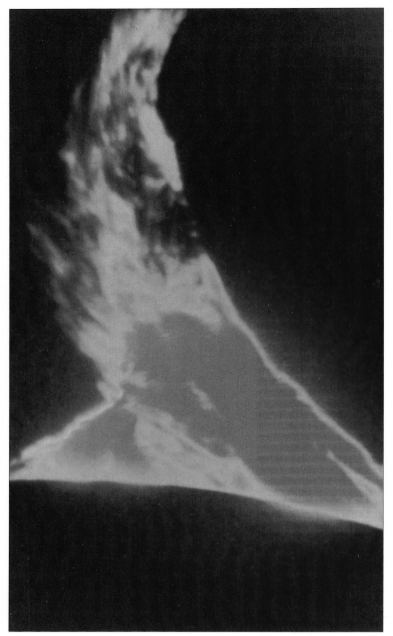

Above A mighty tongue of flame shoots high up above the surface of the Sun. It is a solar flare. Flares occur suddenly and without warning. They let loose great amounts of energy with explosive force. They give out radiation and streams of atomic particles. But they do not last long – often for only a few minutes.

The solar wind

The Sun not only gives off light and heat, it also gives off atomic particles. These flow away from the Sun, forming what is called the solar wind.

When the particles come near the Earth, some get trapped in its magnetic field. They form ring-shaped regions in space called the Van Allen belts.

When there are lots of sunspots or flares on the Sun, the solar wind blows strongly. It causes Earth's magnetic field to change slightly. Then we say a magnetic storm has occurred.

The strong solar wind also knocks particles from

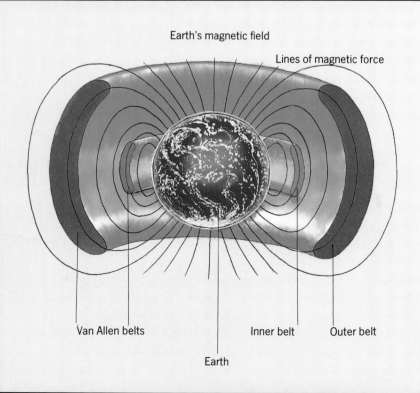

Earth's magnetic field

Lines of magnetic force

Van Allen belts

Inner belt

Outer belt

Earth

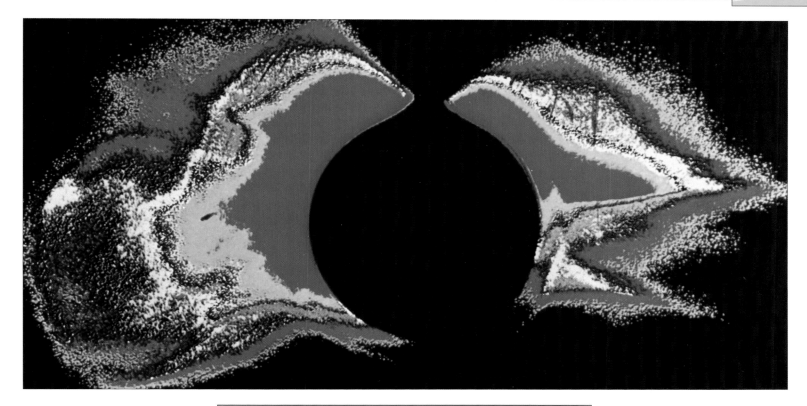

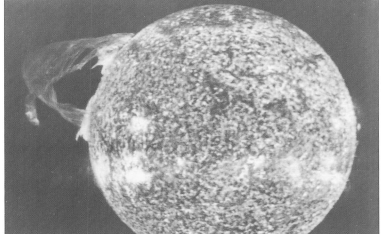

Above This spectacular picture shows the Sun's corona, its thin outer atmosphere. It was taken by astronauts aboard Skylab in 1973. They had caused an artificial eclipse with an instrument called a coronagraph. The different colours show up different levels of brightness.

Left The Skylab astronauts also photographed this gigantic prominence on the Sun. Like most prominences it curved up and over in a spectacular loop, which follows the direction of the Sun's powerful magnetic field. In all it has leapt some 700,000 km across the solar surface.

the Van Allen Belts. They rain down into the atmosphere and collide with the air particles, making them give off light. From the ground we see the light as shimmering curtains, and call it the aurora. Aurorae are seen mostly in far northern and far southern parts of the world, where they are called the Northern and Southern Lights.

Right At times when the Sun is very active, radios and televisions are affected on Earth. **Below** Astronauts aboard the space shuttle in 1985 photographed the Aurora Borealis from above.

THE PLANETS

Over the following pages, we shall look at the nine planets in our Solar System in more detail. We will deal with them in the order of their distance from the Sun, beginning with Mercury and ending with Pluto.

From the Earth we can see five of the other planets without needing to use a telescope: Mercury, Venus, Mars, Jupiter and Saturn. They look like bright stars. But while stars appear fixed in space, planets change their positions among the star patterns ('constellations') from month to month. That is why ancient astronomers called them planets: the word means 'wanderers'.

Through a telescope, the planets look quite different from stars. They show up as a disc rather than just as a point. Powerful telescopes are needed to see the three most distant planets: Uranus, Neptune and Pluto. So ancient astronomers knew nothing about them.

We now know an enormous amount about the planets, thanks to space probes (see page 84). They have travelled hundreds of millions of kilometres into the depths of the Solar System and taken close-up pictures of all the planets except Pluto.

Modelling the solar system

In about 1710, an Englishman named George Graham built a mechanical model of the Solar System. He called it an orrery, after the 4th Earl of Orrery.

An orrery shows how the planets and their moons move. Winding a handle makes the planets circle around a central Sun, and makes moons revolve around the planets.

The orrery was also called a planetarium. Today we use the word planetarium as the name for a building in which the night sky is projected on a domed ceiling.

This elegant French 'planetarium' was made in about 1790.

Below The nine planets in their orbits around the Sun. The inner part of the Solar System has been expanded to show the positions of the four rocky terrestrial (Earth-like) planets. The four big outer planets are giant gas balls.

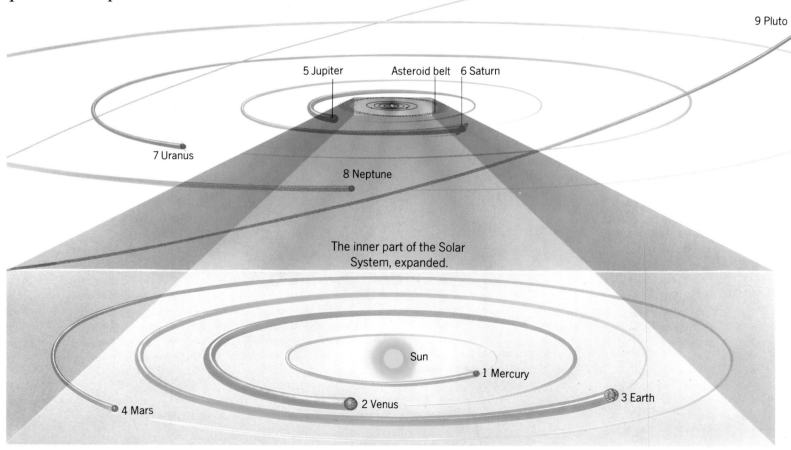

9 Pluto

5 Jupiter   Asteroid belt   6 Saturn

7 Uranus

8 Neptune

The inner part of the Solar System, expanded.

Sun

1 Mercury

4 Mars   2 Venus   3 Earth

MERCURY

Mercury, which is the second smallest planet, is not much bigger than the Moon. It also looks much like the Moon, being covered with craters large and small. These craters were made long, long ago when Mercury was bombarded from space with big lumps of rock. Also like the Moon, the planet has no atmosphere.

Because Mercury lies close to the Sun, it is a very hot world. Temperatures can soar to more than 425°C on the side facing the Sun. This is over four times hotter than boiling water. The surface gets so hot because the planet spins very slowly as it circles the Sun. So parts of the surface stay exposed to the scorching heat of the Sun for three Earth-months at a time.

Mercury is difficult to see from the Earth because it stays so close to the Sun in the sky. But we can see it in some months low on the horizon at sunset or sunrise.

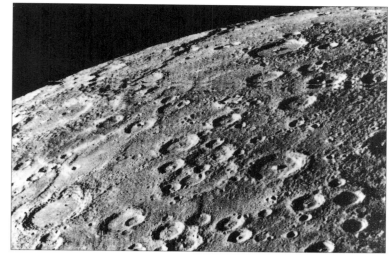

Above Thousands of craters scar the surface of Mercury. This photograph shows part of the northern hemisphere of the planet. It was taken by the space probe Mariner 10 from a height of 78,000 km. Mercury travels faster than any other planet, at about 180,000 km an hour.

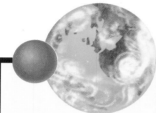

MERCURY

Diameter
at equator: 4,878 km
Mass
(Earth = 1): 0.06 (about 1/17)
Volume
(Earth = 1): 0.05 (1/20)
Density
(water = 1): 5.4
Distance
from Sun: 58,000,000 km
Orbits
the Sun in: 88 days
Spins
on axis in: 58 days 16 hours
Temperature
highest: 450°C
lowest: −183°C
Moons
0

Atmosphere

None

Structure

Crust
Mantle

Iron-rich core

Spying on Mercury

We can see hardly any details on Mercury from the Earth, even through a telescope. But in 1974 and 1975 a NASA probe named Mariner 10 flew past the planet three times, taking thousands of close-up pictures.

Mariner 10 was launched from Earth in November 1973, and flew first to Venus. There, Venus's gravity made it move faster and flung it towards Mercury. It was the first time that this gravity-assist method had been used.

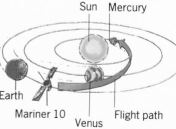

Sun Mercury

Earth

Mariner 10 Venus Flight path

Left Mariner 10 used TV cameras to take pictures of Mercury. This is a mosaic of images obtained in 1974.

VENUS

On many nights of the year a bright star appears in the western sky at sunset, but soon disappears. We call it the evening star. However, it is not a star but the planet Venus. At other times Venus shines brightly in the eastern sky at sunrise, when we call it the morning star.

After the Moon, Venus is the brightest object in the night sky. It shines brightly because it is the planet that comes closest to the Earth. Also, it is covered with dense white clouds, which reflect sunlight brilliantly.

Venus is only slightly smaller than the Earth. Like Earth, it is made mainly of rock and has a cloudy atmosphere. But in other ways it is nothing like our planet.

Venus is a dreadful world, with a thick, suffocating atmosphere that would crush a human being. The temperature at the surface is 480°C or more, and the pressure of the atmosphere is over 90 times that on Earth. The atmosphere is made up mainly of carbon dioxide gas, in which clouds of sulphuric acid swirl. It traps the Sun's heat like a greenhouse, making Venus twice as hot as an oven.

Above Swirling clouds in the atmosphere of Venus show up in this image, sent back by the Mariner 10 probe in 1974. The picture was taken in ultraviolet light, which shows up the cloud formations.

The Phases of Venus

From the Earth we see different views of Venus as it travels in its orbit around the Sun. We see it as a whole disc for only a short time, when it is on the opposite side of the Sun. Mostly, we see only a part-disc. We call the changes in appearance of Venus its phases.

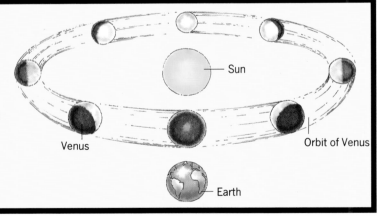

Sun

Venus

Orbit of Venus

Earth

Below The surface of Venus is littered with rocks. Many have been split by the furnace-like heat. The Russian probe Venera 13 sent back this picture in 1982, soon after it had landed on the surface. The probe was crushed to pieces two hours after landing.

The globe (left) shows the surface of Venus in three dimensions. It was made using readings sent back by the Pioneer Venus probe, which went into orbit around the planet in 1978. Pioneer Venus used radar to see through the thick clouds that normally block our view of the surface. The highest region on the globe (orange) forms one of the two great continents on Venus, called Aphrodite Terra. It is about the size of Africa. The other main continent, Ishtar Terra, is shown on the map of Venus below. Most of the planet consists of low plains.

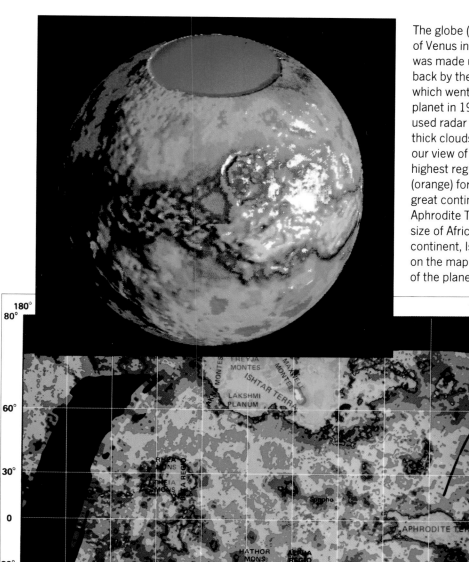

VENUS

Diameter
at equator: 12,104 km
Mass
(Earth = 1): 0.8
Volume
(Earth = 1): 0.9
Density
(water = 1): 5.2
Distance
from Sun: 108,000,000 km
Orbits
the Sun in: 224 days 17 hours
Spins
on axis in: 243 days 4 hours
Temperature
surface average: 480°C
Moons
0

Atmosphere

Haze

Main cloud
layer

Carbon
dioxide gas

Structure

Crust

Mantle

Rocky core

Mapping with Magellan

In 1990 and 1991 NASA's Magellan spacecraft mapped most of Venus in great detail. It used radar to peer through the cloud and produce detailed images of the surface, like the one below.

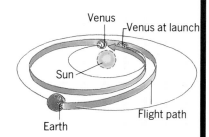

Venus
Venus at launch
Sun
Flight path
Earth

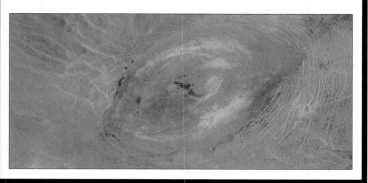

Colonizing Venus

Some scientists think that it might one day be possible to turn Venus into another Earth. They call the process terraforming. The plan would be to drop primitive plants called algae into the atmosphere. These would gobble up the carbon dioxide there, and give off oxygen as a waste product. In time the atmosphere would thin out, allowing trapped heat to escape. Rain would start to fall on the cooling planet. After many centuries, humans might be able to land and start a colony.

PLANET EARTH

The third planet out from the Sun is our home, the Earth. In some ways it is like the other planets. It spins on its own axis like a top (once a day) and circles around the Sun (once a year). Like its neighbours in space, Venus and Mars, it is made up of rock. And, like most of the planets, it is surrounded by a layer of gas called an atmosphere.

In other ways, however, the Earth is completely different from the other planets. In particular, it is the home of millions upon millions of living plants and animals. These range in size from germs you can see only under a microscope to huge animals like the blue whale, which grows up to 27 metres long.

As far as we know, the other planets harbour no life of any kind.

The Earth was born as a red-hot ball of molten rock some 4,600 million years ago. In time, the surface cooled down to form a hard crust. Since then it has been constantly changing. At present less than one-third of the Earth's surface is made up of land areas, or continents. More than two-thirds is covered by the water of the oceans.

Millions of years ago the surface continents had different shapes and were in different positions. In millions of years time, they will look different again. This is because they are slowly drifting. They are being carried along on pieces, or plates, of the Earth's crust that are moving in different directions.

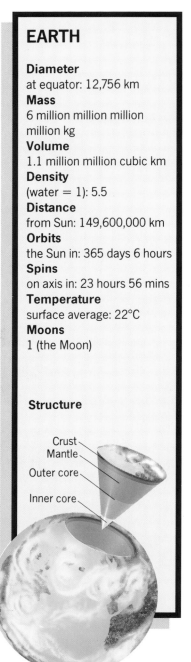

EARTH

Diameter
at equator: 12,756 km
Mass
6 million million million million kg
Volume
1.1 million million cubic km
Density
(water = 1): 5.5
Distance
from Sun: 149,600,000 km
Orbits
the Sun in: 365 days 6 hours
Spins
on axis in: 23 hours 56 mins
Temperature
surface average: 22°C
Moons
1 (the Moon)

Structure

Crust
Mantle
Outer core
Inner core

Left Rain clouds gather over the rolling countryside. Clouds form when water vapour comes out of the atmosphere as tiny water droplets. In rain clouds, the droplets collide with one another, grow bigger and fall out of the cloud as rain.

Right A section through the Earth's atmosphere, which is made up mainly of the gases nitrogen and oxygen. The air gets thinner the higher up you go. We can divide up the atmosphere into layers. The air is thickest in the bottom layer, the troposphere, which is where our weather occurs. The next layer is the stratosphere. Within it is a layer of ozone, which filters out dangerous rays from sunlight. Next comes the ionosphere. There, the few particles of air left exist as ions (charged atoms). In this layer meteors burn up and displays of the Northern and Southern lights occur. Beyond the ionosphere is the final layer of atmosphere, the exosphere. This gradually merges into space.

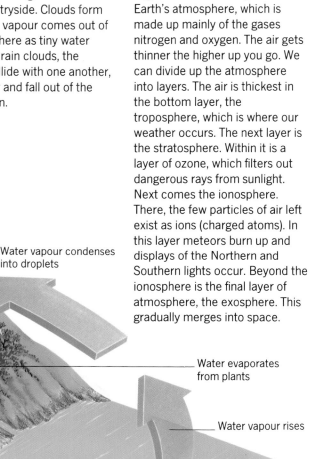

Clouds

Water vapour condenses into droplets

Water drops fall as rain

Water evaporates from plants

Water vapour rises

Water evaporates from ocean

Water runs back to ocean

Above The never-ending water cycle on Earth. Water evaporates (turns to vapour) from the oceans. Plants give off water vapour too. Clouds of water droplets form as the vapour rises and cools. Water falls back to the ground as rain or snow.

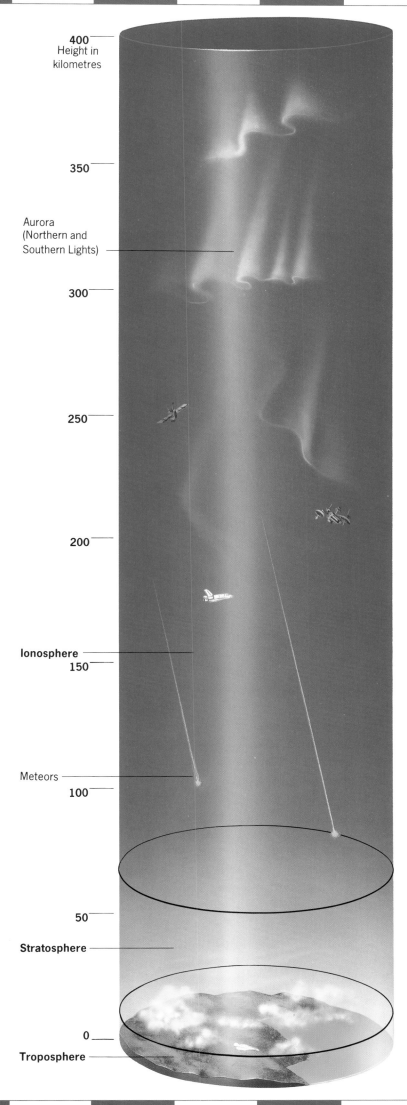

400
Height in
kilometres

350

Aurora
(Northern and
Southern Lights)

300

250

200

Ionosphere
150

Meteors

100

50

Stratosphere

0

Troposphere

The Greenhouse effect

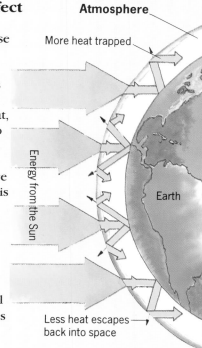

Atmosphere

More heat trapped

Gardeners use a greenhouse to raise plants that need warm conditions. The greenhouse traps the Sun's heat. The atmosphere also traps some of the Sun's heat, but most escapes back into space. However, more and more carbon dioxide is getting into the atmosphere from the fuels we burn. This is causing a 'greenhouse effect', making the atmosphere trap more of the Sun's heat.

As a result, the world is getting warmer. If it gets too warm, our weather will change. The ice at the Poles will start to melt, causing widespread flooding.

Energy from the Sun

Earth

Less heat escapes back into space

Right Ammonite fossils. Life began in the sea millions of years ago. Ammonites, very early shellfish, lived 140 million years ago, Ammonite fossils found in layers of rock in Europe and North America provide evidence that these continents were once submerged under oceans.

Right The famous Grand Canyon in the western United States. This huge gash in the ground was cut by the Colorado River over thousands of years. Flowing water is one of the main things that changes the face of the Earth.

Below Mount Etna, in Sicily, erupts in a glorious natural firework display in 1971. As far as we know, Earth is the only planet that has active volcanoes.

THE EARTH: CLIMATE AND LIFE

The Earth provides just the right conditions for life as we know it to thrive. Because of its position in the Solar System, it is neither too hot, nor too cold. Its atmosphere contains the oxygen living things need to breathe. And there is plenty of water for them to drink.

Different plants and animals are found in different parts of the world. This happens mainly because every living thing grows best in a certain climate or pattern of weather. And there are several kinds of climates, or patterns of weather, throughout the world.

The two main features of a climate are the temperature (how hot) and the rainfall (how wet). The hottest climates are found around the Equator, in the so-called tropics. Some parts of the tropics also have the highest rainfall – up to 10 metres a year! Plants thrive in such hot, wet climates, and they provide food for a great variety of animals.

Just north and south of the tropics are vast desert regions, which can be very hot (40°C or more) but very dry. In the desert it is harder for animals and plants to survive. Farther north and south still, climates get cooler but there is enough rain to support rich plant life. These are the temperate regions.

Nearer to the North and South Poles, the climate becomes very cold indeed. In temperatures as low as −50°C, life again becomes a struggle for plants and animals.

Above The climate of the Arctic is harsh. Few animals can survive there. Thick fur with a layer of blubber underneath protect polar bears from the extreme cold.

Below Northern forests are wetter and warmer than the Arctic. This moose will find plenty to eat.

NORTH AMERICA

ATLANTIC OCEAN

Equator

SOUTH AMERICA

Concentrated heat

The Earth is shaped like a spinning globe which bulges out in the middle. The Equator receives the direct, highly concentrated rays of the Sun all year. It is the hottest zone on Earth. Away from the Equator, the Sun hits the earth at an angle. This means the sunlight is less concentrated and the temperature is not as high as at the Equator.

Area of surface covered by beam

Earth

North

Beams of sunlight

Equator

South

KEY

Cold lands

Mountains

Northern forest

Temperate forest

Tropical forest

Grassland

Desert

The Seasons

The angle at which the Earth is tilted toward the Sun as it revolves around it determines which season it will be. This means that when the North Pole is tilted toward the Sun the northern hemisphere has its summer and the southern hemisphere has its winter. When the South Pole is tilted toward the Sun it is

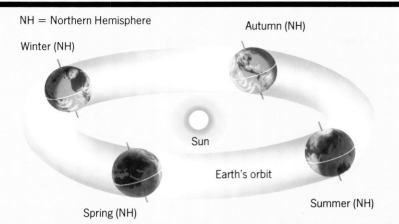

NH = Northern Hemisphere

Winter (NH)

Autumn (NH)

Sun

Earth's orbit

Spring (NH)

Summer (NH)

summer in the southern hemisphere and winter in the northern hemisphere.

When it is autumn in the southern hemisphere, it is spring in the northern hemisphere.

This diagram shows the tilt of the Earth for each season in the northern hemisphere. Where the North Pole is tilted furthest away from the Sun it is winter.

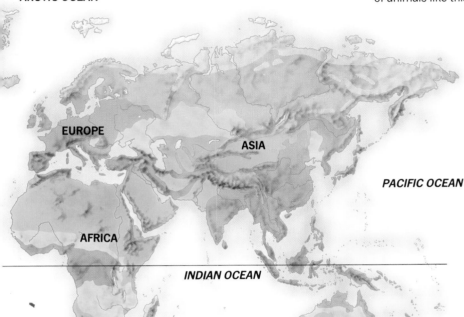

ARCTIC OCEAN

EUROPE

ASIA

PACIFIC OCEAN

AFRICA

INDIAN OCEAN

AUSTRALIA

Right Temperate forests get lots of rain and are home to a variety of animals like this fallow deer.

Below Tropical rainforests are moist and warm all year and provide a home for many species. Lemurs live in the trees eating fruit and insects.

Above Deserts are the driest zones on Earth. Very hot during the day, deserts can be extremely cold at night. Camels can survive several days without water, and can withstand both the hot and cold temperatures of the desert.

Left Grasslands are dry, hot, wide open places. Thick grass covers the soil. In the short rainy season everything bursts into bloom and dies down again quickly in the heat. Kangaroos are grass-eaters who can survive on very little water. They use their powerful hind legs to sprint away if they see a predator off in the distance.

THE MOON

The Earth travels through space with a close companion, the Moon. The Moon is about 100 times closer to us than the nearest planet, Venus. It is the Earth's only natural satellite, and travels around the Earth about once a month. It is quite a small body, with only about one-quarter of the diameter of the Earth.

Like the Earth, the Moon is made up of rock. But it is quite unlike our own planet in most other ways. It has no air, no water, no plants, no animals. It is a silent, dry, grey world. We know this for certain because astronauts have visited the Moon and explored its surface.

The Moon shines brightly in the sky on most nights, but it does not give out light of its own. It shines only by reflecting the light from the Sun. Because of this, we see different parts of the Moon lit up at different times as it circles around the Earth once a month. We call these changes in the Moon's appearance its phases.

At the time of the Full Moon, we see the complete face, or disc, of the Moon lit up. Then even without a telescope, we can make out some details on the disc, such as dark areas and light areas. Through binoculars or a telescope, we can see that the dark areas are great flat plains. We call them 'seas', but there is no water in them. The light areas are rugged highlands or mountain chains.

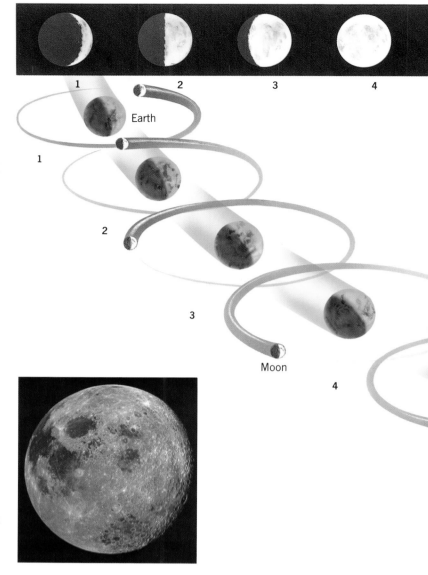

Above Apollo astronauts took this picture of the Moon in 1972. It is a different view from the one we see from Earth. The easiest feature to recognize is the circular Sea of Crises.

Below The Full Moon seen from Earth. The dark areas are flat plains, which we call seas, or maria. The bright crater near the bottom is Tycho.

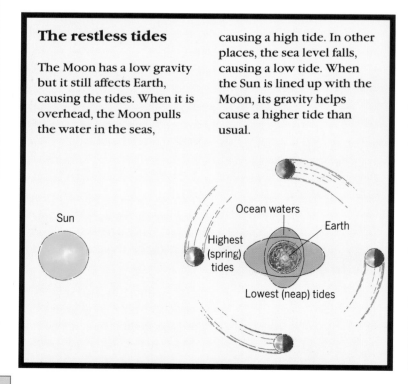

The restless tides

The Moon has a low gravity but it still affects Earth, causing the tides. When it is overhead, the Moon pulls the water in the seas, causing a high tide. In other places, the sea level falls, causing a low tide. When the Sun is lined up with the Moon, its gravity helps cause a higher tide than usual.

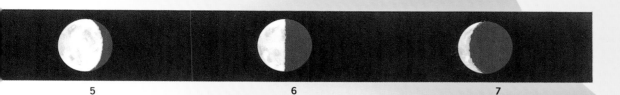

5   6   7

Sun

The pictures above show the phases of the Moon. The diagrams below show how these come about. Different amounts of the Moon's surface are lit by sunlight as it travels along its orbit round the Earth.

At the phase of the New Moon, we cannot see the Moon at all. It is between us and the Sun and only its far side is lit up. A few days later, the Moon has moved along its orbit, and we see a thin crescent (1). A week after New Moon, half of the Moon is lit up (2, First Quarter phase). Then more and more is lit up (3, gibbous Moon), until the whole disc shines (4) at Full Moon.

The amount of surface lit up then gradually gets smaller (5, gibbous Moon), to half-circle (6, Last Quarter) and crescent (7). The Moon disappears at the next New Moon, 29½ days after the last one.

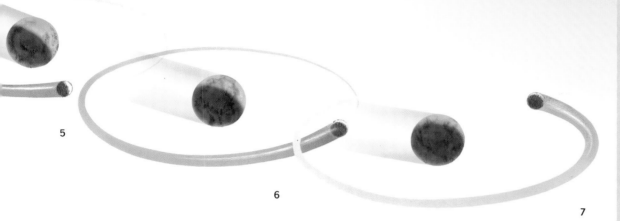

5   6   7

THE MOON

Diameter
at equator: 3,476 km
Mass
(Earth = 1): 0.0123 (1/81)
Volume
(Earth = 1): 0.0203 (1/49)
Density
(water = 1): 3.3
Distance
from Earth: 384,000 km
Orbits
the Earth in: 27 days 8 hours
Spins
on axis in: 27 days 8 hours
Phases
29 days 13 hours
Temperature
highest: 120°C
lowest: −160°C

Atmosphere

None

Structure

Crust —
Mantle —
Iron-rich core

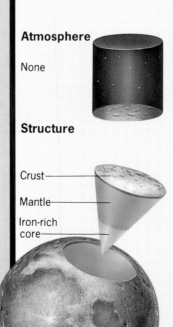

Below The far side of the Moon, which we can never see from the Earth. This is because, as the Moon circles around the Earth, it also spins round slowly and keeps the same face towards us. The far side looks quite different from the near side because it has no large seas. The small sea near the limb at bottom right is the Eastern Sea. The sea at top left is the Sea of Moscow.

Lunatics and werewolves

Ancient peoples worshipped the Moon. In mythology, the Roman goddess Diana used the crescent Moon as a bow and moonbeams as arrows.

People were also very superstitious about the Moon, thinking they would go mad if they gazed at it too long. Our word lunatic, comes from the Latin word for Moon, *luna*. At Full Moon people believed that some men could turn into savage killer werewolves.

The first and last Apollo landings took place in this hemisphere of the Moon (see page 88).

In July 1969 Apollo II landed near the southern edge of the Sea of Tranquillity. On July 20 Neil Armstrong and Edwin Aldrin planted the first human footsteps in the lunar soil.

The last mission, Apollo 17, went to a site near the edge of the Sea of Serenity. It ended on December 14, 1972. In between there were four other landings. In all, 12 astronauts explored the Moon and brought back 385 kg of Moon rocks.

Above The Apollo 11 lunar module rises into lunar orbit after the first Moon landing. It is about to dock with the Apollo mother ship. Far below is one of the Moon's smaller seas, Smith's Sea. Hanging in the sky is planet Earth.

Below On the Apollo 17 mission astronaut Harrison Schmitt gets down to some lunar gardening. What he is actually doing is collecting rock chips. The Apollo 17 astronauts spent over 22 hours exploring the Moon.

THE MOON: EASTERN HEMISPHERE

The map opposite shows the eastern half, or hemisphere, of the side of the Moon that faces us. The seas and craters named are the ones easiest to see. The map is drawn with north at the top, south at the bottom, west to the left and east to the right. It shows the Moon the right way up, as you would view it with your eyes and through binoculars. If you look at the Moon through a telescope, however, you will see it the other way up, with south at the top.

The easiest feature to spot in this hemisphere of the Moon is the circular Sea of Crises near the eastern edge. Farther west are three much larger seas joined together. They are the Seas of Serenity, Tranquillity and Fertility. It was on the Sea of Tanquillity that people from planet Earth first set foot on the Moon in July 1969 (see page 88). At the western edge of the Sea of Serenity are the Apennine Mountains.

Above This photograph shows a valley cutting through the lunar Alps in the north of this hemisphere. Called Alpine Valley, it runs for about 130 km. The channel running along the bottom of the valley looks like the course of a river, but it can't be. No water has ever flowed on the Moon. The plain on the left of the picture is the Sea of Showers.

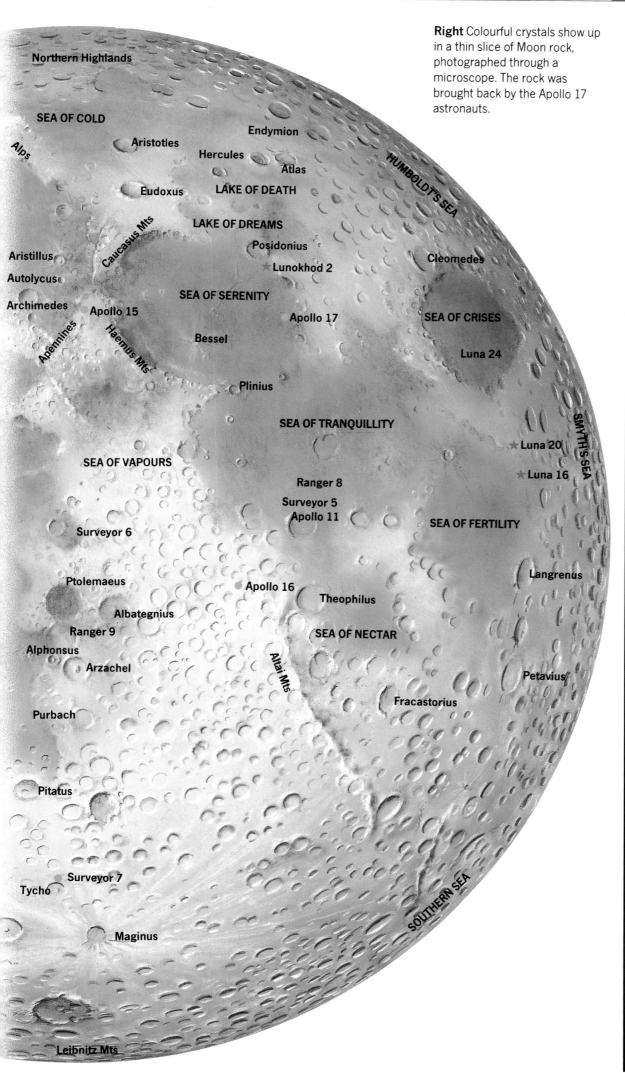

Northern Highlands

SEA OF COLD

Alps

Aristotles

Endymion

Eudoxus

Hercules

Atlas

LAKE OF DEATH

Caucasus Mts

LAKE OF DREAMS

HUMBOLDT'S SEA

Aristillus

Posidonius

Autolycus

★ Lunokhod 2

Cleomedes

Archimedes

SEA OF SERENITY

Apollo 15

Apollo 17

SEA OF CRISES

Haemus Mts

Bessel

Luna 24

Apennines

Plinius

SEA OF TRANQUILLITY

SMYTH'S SEA

SEA OF VAPOURS

★ Luna 20

Ranger 8

★ Luna 16

Surveyor 5

Surveyor 6

Apollo 11

SEA OF FERTILITY

Ptolemaeus

Apollo 16

Langrenus

Albategnius

Theophilus

Ranger 9

SEA OF NECTAR

Alphonsus

Arzachel

Petavius

Altai Mts

Purbach

Fracastorius

Pitatus

Surveyor 7

Tycho

SOUTHERN SEA

Maginus

Leibnitz Mts

Right Colourful crystals show up in a thin slice of Moon rock, photographed through a microscope. The rock was brought back by the Apollo 17 astronauts.

KEY FEATURES

Arzachel Crater 80 km across, 2,365 m deep.
Atlas Crater 87 km in diameter with terraced walls and complex floor.
Caucasus Mountains Rugged mountains which reach a height of 3,657 m in places.
Cleomedes Walled plain 125 km in diameter in the Sea of Crises with high ramparts.
Eudoxus Large crater 64 km in diameter, with 3,350 m high walls.
Langrenus Bright walled plain 132 km in diameter. It is also a ray centre.
Plinius Crater 48 km in diameter separating the Sea of Serenity from the Sea of Tranquillity. Contains a smaller double crater.
Posidonius Walled plain 99 km across with worn down and broken walls.
Ptolemaeus Walled plain 150 km in diameter. Central peaks rise up to 2,745 m.
Sea of Crises Circular sea 500 km across which can be seen with the naked eye. The smooth interior has three well-marked craters.
Sea of Fertility Irregularly shaped mare about 1,000 km across.
Sea of Serenity A circular mare about 600 km across.
Sea of Tranquillity Site of 'Tranquillity Base' where the Apollo 11 astronauts landed on July 20, 1969. It is a lowland 650 × 900 km.
Theophilus Crater over 100 km in diameter with terraced walls rising to 5,485 m.

KEY FEATURES

Apennine Mountains
Range containing peaks up to 4,572 m high.

Aristarchus Young crater 45 km in diameter.

Bay of Rainbows Large bay 260 km in diameter on the Sea of Showers. Part of its walls are the Jura Mountains.

Copernicus Crater over 3,000 m deep and 90 km in diameter. Its rays spread out over 600 km.

Gassendi Partially flooded ring 100 km in diameter.

Grimaldi Dark-floored enclosure with a diameter of 222 km. Some peaks in its walls reach 2,438 m high.

Kepler Crater and major ray centre 32 km in diameter with heavily terraced walls.

Ocean of Storms Vast dark plain, the largest mare region on the Moon. It covers an area of over 5 million square km.

Plato Dark-floored crater 96 km in diameter with walls up to 1,220 m high.

Schickard Dark-floored enclosure 227 km in diameter.

Schiller Enclosure 179 × 71 km shaped like a footprint.

Sea of Showers Sea covering an area over 647,475 square km, with a diameter of 1,040 km.

Sea of Vapours Lowland plain 420 km across.

Tycho Crater 86 km in diameter with massive walls. Rays from Tycho extend over 1,500 km in all directions.

Northern Highlands

SEA OF COLD

Aristotles

Plato

Alps

Eudoxus

Jura Mts

BAY OF RAINBOWS

Caucasus Mts

Lunokhod 1

Aristillus

Autolycus

SEA OF SHOWERS

Archimedes

Apollo 15

Aristarchus

Apennines

SEA OF VAPOURS

Luna 13

Carpathians

Eratosthenes

OCEAN OF STORMS

Kepler

Copernicus

Luna 9

Surveyor 6

Equator

Surveyor 3

Apollo 14

Apollo 12

Albategnius

Surveyor 1

Ptolemaeus

Grimaldi

Ranger 7

Ranger 9

Alphonsus

SEA OF CLOUDS

Arzachel

Cordillera Mts

Purbach

Gassendi

SEA OF MOISTURE

Pitatus

Surveyor 7

Tycho

Rock Mts

Schickard

Longomontanus

Maginus

Schiller

Clavius

Leibnitz Mts

Left A sample of Moon rock from the Apollo 15 landing site in the foothills of the Apennine mountain range. It is a typical volcanic rock, riddled with gas holes.

THE MOON: WESTERN HEMISPHERE

The map opposite shows the western hemisphere of the nearside of the Moon. Most of this hemisphere is covered by vast seas. In the north is the circular Sea of Showers, which is ringed by mountain ranges. It is separated by the lofty Apennine Mountains from the Sea of Serenity in the eastern hemisphere. In the south the Sea of Showers merges with the sprawling Ocean of Storms, the largest of the lunar seas.

At the time of the Full Moon, two large craters, Copernicus and Kepler, show up brilliantly in the Ocean of Storms. And sparkling white rays radiate from them, like spokes from the hub of a bicycle wheel. In the south bright rays surround the small but spectacular crater Tycho.

Full Moon is not the best time to see most features. Craters and mountains show up best at other times, particularly when they are near the 'terminator'. This is the boundary between the light and dark parts of the surface.

Apollo science

The Apollo astronauts carried out experiments at each of the landing sites. And at each site except the first, they also set up a scientific station. This was made up of a variety of instruments, a nuclear battery to power them, and a radio to send results back to Earth.

Together, the equipment was known as ALSEP, the Apollo Lunar Surface Experiments Package. The

Above Apollo 16 astronaut John Young poses next to the ALSEP scientific station he and fellow moonwalker Charles Duke have set up.

instruments included a seismometer, a device to record ground tremors, or 'moonquakes'. Other instruments measured the Moon's magnetism and recorded the atomic particles bombarding the Moon from outer space.

Right The crater Eratosthenes dominates this Moonscape. It is a well-formed crater, measuring about 65 km across. Like many lunar craters, it has a small mountain range in the middle. Eratosthenes lies on the edge of the Apennine mountain range. In the picture, a plain stretches beyond the crater to the horizon. It is the Sea of Showers, the largest of the circular seas.

SHADOWS IN SPACE

When you stand in the sunlight, you cast a dark shadow on the ground. In a similar way, but on a much larger scale, the Earth and the Moon cast dark shadows in space. Sometimes, as the Moon circles around the Earth, it moves into the Earth's shadow. And it more or less disappears from view. We call this event an eclipse of the Moon, or a lunar eclipse.

Sometimes the Moon moves between the Sun and the Earth and casts its own shadow on the Earth. In the shadow, the face of the Sun is blotted out. We call this event an eclipse of the Sun, or a solar eclipse. Only a few lunar and solar eclipses take place each year. Lunar eclipses occur at a Full Moon, solar eclipses at a New Moon.

If the Moon covers only part of the Sun's face, we call it a partial solar eclipse. If the Sun is completely covered, we call it a total eclipse. Seeing a total eclipse is very exciting. Daylight gradually turns into twilight, which suddenly fades into darkness. After a few minutes, twilight and then daylight return as the Moon's shadow passes by.

Astronomers travel all around the world to observe total eclipses. This is because at such times they can see and study the Sun's outer atmosphere (see page 14).

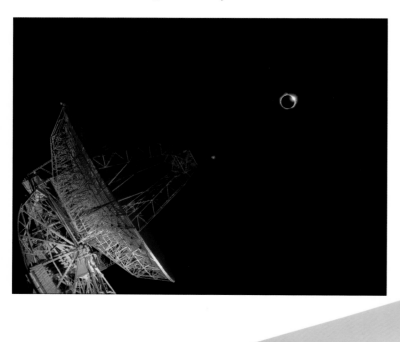

Left A dramatic picture taken on Wallops Island, Virginia, USA, during a total eclipse of the Sun in March 1970. In the foreground is an aerial for tracking spacecraft. The eclipse is in its 'diamond-ring' stage and will soon be over.

Orbit of Moon

Earth

Total eclipse

Moon

Moon's shadow

Light from the Sun

Above An eclipse of the Sun happens when the Moon passes across the Sun's face. The dark shadow (umbra) cast by the Moon at total eclipse is never more than 270 km wide. Outside is a larger region of lighter shadow (penumbra), where a partial eclipse is seen.

Swallowing the Sun

These days we know when eclipses of the Sun will take place. Today eclipses of the Sun can be forecast ahead using calculations. Most ancient people were terrified when a solar eclipse occurred without any warning. The Chinese thought that the Sun was being swallowed by a dragon. So they banged gongs and drums to frighten it and make it cough up the Sun. This always worked.

Earth's shadow

Eclipse of the Moon

Orbit of Earth

Total solar eclipse
Bangka Island, Indonesia, March 18, 1988

Right The eclipse is well under way. The Moon is covering over a quarter of the Sun.

Above Seconds before totality, the Moon's shadow is racing past the eclipse observers. The horizon turns orange.

Right The eclipse is now total, and the corona lights up. This is the Sun's outer atmosphere, which we normally can't see because the face of the Sun is so bright. The corona extends several million kilometres into space.

Right Only about two minutes after the Sun's face was hidden by the Moon, it is about to emerge again. But there are spectacles still to come. Vivid pink prominences appear: they are fountains of hot gas leaping up from the surface of the Sun.

Above An eclipse of the Moon takes place when the Moon moves into the Earth's shadow in space. The Moon doesn't completely disappear from view but turns copper-coloured. This is because of sunlight being refracted (bent) on to the surface by the Earth's atmosphere.

Right This is a solar eclipse photographed by the Apollo 12 astronauts on their way back from the second Moon landing in 1969. The astronauts saw the Sun eclipsed by the Earth, not the Moon. Notice how the Sun has lit up the thin layer of atmosphere around the limb of the Earth.

MARS, THE RED PLANET

After Venus, Mars is the planet that comes closest to the Earth. It is one of the easiest planets to spot in the night sky because of its reddish-orange colour. We often call it the Red Planet. This is a good name because space probes have shown that the whole planet is a rusty red colour.

Mars has two tiny moons, called Phobos and Deimos. They are potato-shaped lumps of rock, pitted with craters. Even the biggest, Phobos, is only about 28 kilometres across.

In some ways Mars is similar to the Earth. Its 'day' is only a little longer than our own. It has

Above Mars, as viewed through a powerful telescope from Earth. Dark markings show up on parts of the surface. At the bottom, the white patch is the ice cap at Mars's south pole.

Right A map showing the surface of Mars between latitudes 65 degrees north and south. The most striking features are the four large dead volcanoes, Mariner Valley, and the plain Hellas.

Below This picture is based on photographs of the Martian surface taken by the Viking space probes. It covers much of the area shown in the map. It has been printed in false colours to bring out the relief, or differences in height, of the landscape. Pale blue is lowest; red is highest.

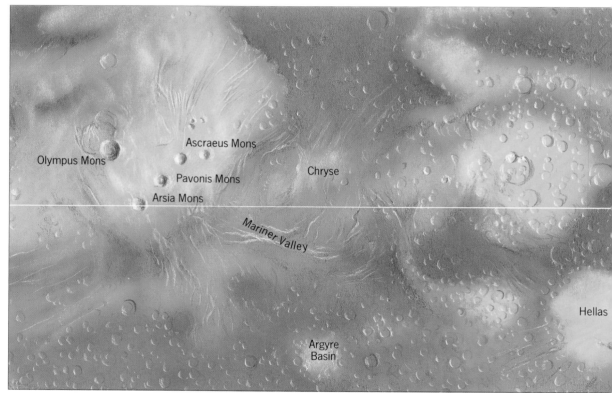

Olympus Mons
Ascraeus Mons
Pavonis Mons
Arsia Mons
Chryse
Mariner Valley
Argyre Basin
Hellas

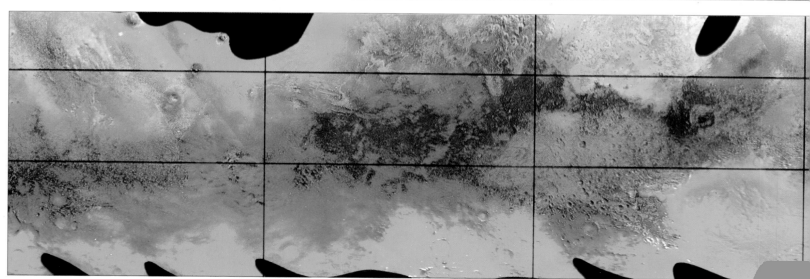

seasons. There are ice caps at its north and south poles. And it has an atmosphere in which clouds form and dust storms rage.

People once thought that conditions on Mars might be suitable for some forms of life, even for intelligent creatures like ourselves. But we now know that the Martian climate is too harsh for any form of life as we know it. For most of the time, temperatures are far lower than they are in polar regions on Earth in winter. Also, there is hardly any atmosphere, and it has no oxygen for breathing.

However, Mars is the only planet in our Solar System on which human astronauts could safely land and explore. Early next century they probably will.

The dying Martians

In 1877 an Italian astronomer named Giovanni Schiaparelli was observing Mars. He said he could see a series of lines criss-crossing the planet. He called these 'canali', meaning 'channels'.

Other people thought of them as real canals – in other words, waterways dug by intelligent beings. One of these people was the noted American astronomer Percival Lowell, who built an observatory in Arizona, to observe Mars better.

Lowell convinced many others that there was an intelligent Martian race desperately building canals, to carry precious water from the polar ice caps to the warmer regions near the equator.

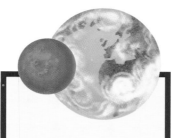

MARS

Diameter
at equator: 6,794 km
Mass
(Earth = 1): 0.11 (about 1/9)
Volume
(Earth = 1): 0.15 (about 1/7)
Density
(water = 1): 3.0
Distance
from Sun: 227,900,000 km
Orbits
the Sun in: 687 days
Spins
on axis in: 24 hours 37 mins
Temperature
average: −23°C
Moons
2

Atmosphere

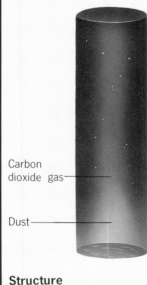

Carbon dioxide gas

Dust

Structure

Crust
Mantle

Rocky core

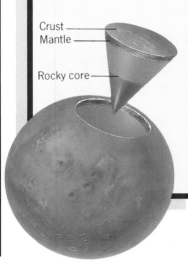

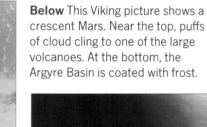

Utopia

Equator

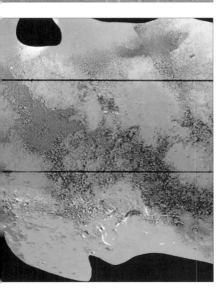

Below This Viking picture shows a crescent Mars. Near the top, puffs of cloud cling to one of the large volcanoes. At the bottom, the Argyre Basin is coated with frost.

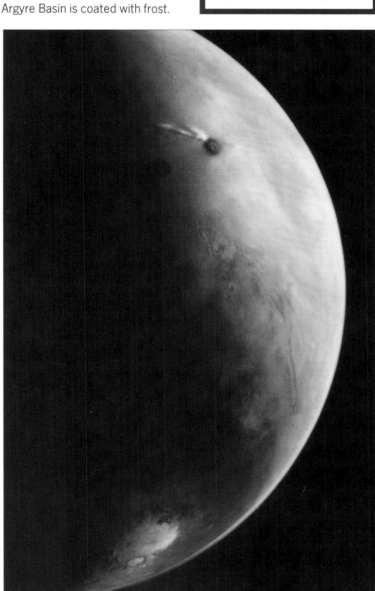

MARS: THE SURFACE

When we look at Mars through a telescope, we can make out only a few dark markings on the surface. But pictures taken by space probes (see page 84) show the surface in great detail.

US Mariner and Viking probes have photographed the whole planet from orbit. The Viking probes have even dropped landers that have set down on the surface. They have sent back close-up pictures and also reported on the Martian weather.

Much of the surface of Mars consists of almost flat plains, which are covered with soil and strewn with rocks large and small. Massive rocks from outer space have crashed into the surface in two places, and carved out two great basins. The largest, called Hellas, measures more than 1,500 kilometres across.

Elsewhere, three huge volcanoes have created a vast highland region, called the Tharsis Ridge. But the highest point of all is the nearby volcano known as Olympus Mons (Mount Olympus). It is twice as high as Earth's highest peak, Mount Everest.

Another spectacular feature on Mars is a great gash in the surface, which we call Mariner Valley. It is a huge canyon that is nearly as long as the Atlantic Ocean is wide.

Above Orange-red rocks and soil cover the surface of the Red Planet. The Viking 1 lander took this close-up picture in a region known as Chryse. Much of the soil is very fine. When the Martian winds blow, they whip up the soil causing huge dust storms.

Below Part of Mariner Valley, which runs across the Martian equator. This Martian 'Grand Canyon' is much bigger than the one on Earth. It is at least 5,000 km long, up to 600 km wide and is 6 km deep in places.

Martian floods

No water flows on Mars today, but some time in the past it almost certainly did. The picture below shows a broad channel, which looks some water channels on Earth after heavy flooding.

Scientists think that on Mars flooding might have come about in this way. Under the surface, there was (and probably still is) water frozen as ice. If the ground was heated, the ice would have melted into water. If this had happened suddenly, flooding would have occurred, with water gouging out channels.

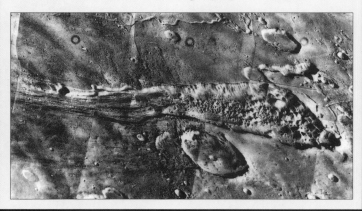

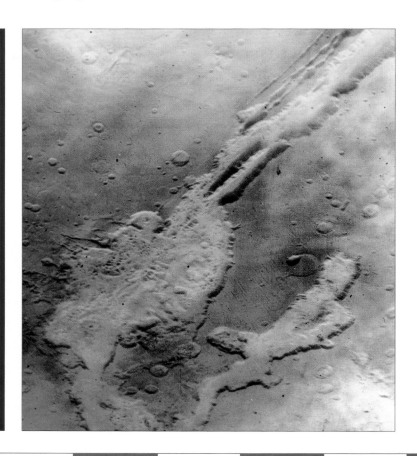

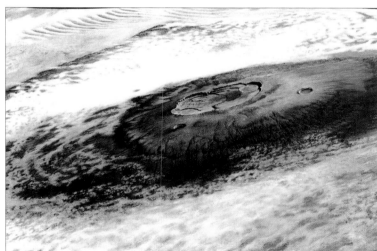

Above The mammoth volcano Olympus Mons (Mount Olympus), wreathed in early morning mist. It rises 25 km above the surrounding plain and is more than 600 km across at the base. The mouth of the crater alone measures over 80 km across.

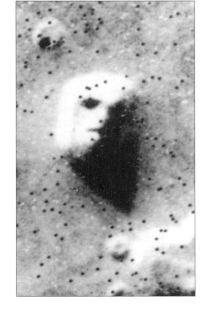

Right A curious rock formation found on Mars, which looks like a head. Some people have suggested it could be a huge sculpture of a Martian face, carved by an ancient civilization on Mars.

The Viking invasion

In 1976, two US space probes called Viking went into orbit around Mars, after a 10-month journey from Earth. First, they swooped over the landscape to check for suitable landing sites. When the sites had been chosen, a lander was dropped to descend to the surface. The rest of the probe continued in orbit.

The Viking 1 lander touched down in a region called Chryse in July. Viking 2 landed in Utopia two months later. Strangely, the pictures they took showed an almost identical-looking landscape at both sites.

The landers both carried a small biological laboratory which tested the soil for signs of life. But no traces of life were found.

Above This Viking lander picture shows part of the probe. Notice the frost patches on the ground.

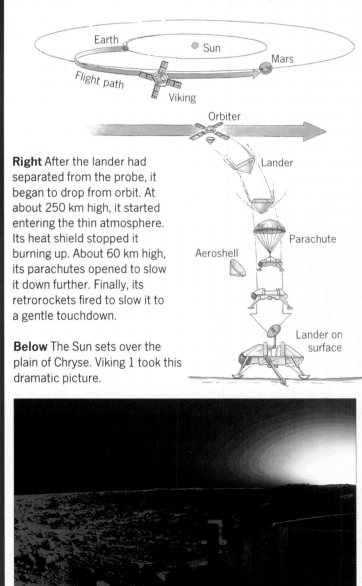

Right After the lander had separated from the probe, it began to drop from orbit. At about 250 km high, it started entering the thin atmosphere. Its heat shield stopped it burning up. About 60 km high, its parachutes opened to slow it down further. Finally, its retrorockets fired to slow it to a gentle touchdown.

Below The Sun sets over the plain of Chryse. Viking 1 took this dramatic picture.

JUPITER: KING OF THE PLANETS

Jupiter is by far the biggest of the planets. It is a giant gas ball that has twice as much mass as all the other planets put together. It could swallow more than 1,300 Earths!

Jupiter is very much farther away than Mars, but often appears much brighter. This is because it is very much bigger and has a cloudy atmosphere that reflects sunlight well.

Through a powerful telescope we can see bands on the face, or disc, of Jupiter. We call the dark ones belts and the light ones zones. Among the bands light and dark spots come and go. We can see them moving across the disc as the planet spins very rapidly on its axis. One spot has been visible for at least three centuries. It is called the Great Red Spot because of its huge size and colour.

Space probes have taken close-up pictures of the belts and zones on the disc. They seem to be clouds that have been pulled out into bands as Jupiter and its atmosphere spin round.

The main gas in the atmosphere is hydrogen, the lightest gas of all. Underneath there is a great ocean of liquid hydrogen tens of thousands of kilometres deep. Right at the centre of the planet there is probably a tiny core of rock. There, the pressure and temperature are very, very high.

Above Jupiter seen through a telescope from Earth. Parallel bands of clouds are visible. And the Great Red Spot shows up clearly in the southern hemisphere. The planet appears oval rather than round. This is because it is made of gas and rotating rapidly. The rapid rotation makes it bulge at the equator.

Below Jupiter seen from 28 million km away, by the Voyager 1 probe. The picture shows colourful bands of clouds and many oval features. These are hurricane-like storm centres. The biggest by far is the Great Red Spot. Two of the four large moons of Jupiter appear in the picture. On the right is Europa, and passing over Jupiter is colourful Io.

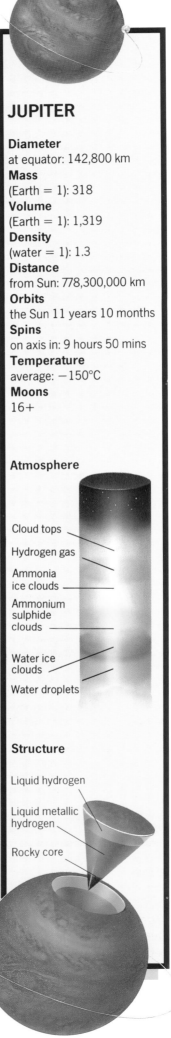

JUPITER

Diameter
at equator: 142,800 km
Mass
(Earth = 1): 318
Volume
(Earth = 1): 1,319
Density
(water = 1): 1.3
Distance
from Sun: 778,300,000 km
Orbits
the Sun 11 years 10 months
Spins
on axis in: 9 hours 50 mins
Temperature
average: −150°C
Moons
16+

Atmosphere

Cloud tops

Hydrogen gas

Ammonia ice clouds

Ammonium sulphide clouds

Water ice clouds

Water droplets

Structure

Liquid hydrogen

Liquid metallic hydrogen

Rocky core

Below This map of Jupiter's northern hemisphere from above was produced from Voyager pictures. The dark patch, over the north pole, shows where no pictures were taken. The belts and zones show up well.

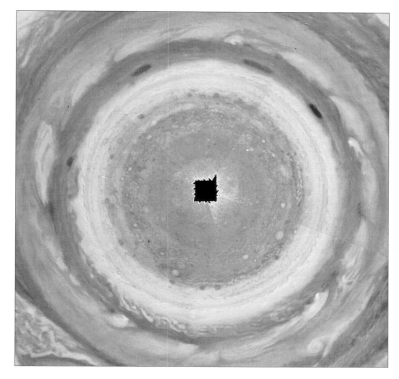

Above A map of Jupiter's southern hemisphere, as pictured from above the south pole. More violent disturbances in the atmosphere occur in southern regions. They are centred on the Great Red Spot.

A failed star?

Jupiter is truly a huge planet. The only thing bigger than Jupiter in the Solar System is the Sun. Earlier this century some astronomers thought that Jupiter did behave like a feeble Sun and give out light of its own. We now know that it does not.

However, Jupiter is in some ways more like a star than a planet. It is made up mainly of hydrogen gas. It has a powerful magnetic field, and it gives off heat, radio waves and even X-rays. This is what stars do.

Perhaps if Jupiter had been much bigger it would have begun to shine as a star.

Belts and zones

Astronomers can make out sets of dark belts and light zones on Jupiter's disc. Their appearance changes from time to time. Each band rotates around the planet at a different speed, depending on its distance north or south of the equator. The equatorial zone rotates fastest, lapping the planet in 9 hours 50 minutes.

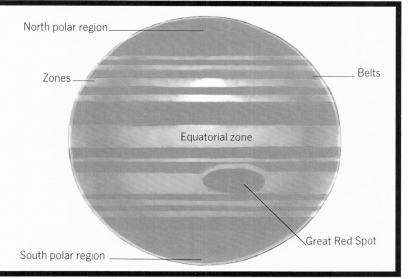

North polar region

Zones

Belts

Equatorial zone

Great Red Spot

South polar region

Right The swirling atmosphere in the region of the Great Red Spot. Astronomers have seen this great storm centre through telescopes on and off for over 300 years. It varies both in size and in colour. At present it measures about 28,000 km long and 14,000 km across.

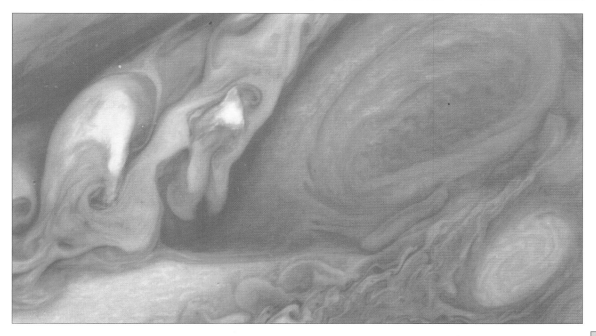

JUPITER: MOONS AND RING

If you look at Jupiter through binoculars, you can usually see up to four bright 'stars' close by. In fact, they are not stars, but the largest of Jupiter's moons. They and at least 12 other moons circle around Jupiter just like our Moon circles around the Earth.

The four large moons are Io, Europa, Ganymede and Callisto, in order of distance from the planet. Ganymede is the biggest moon in the Solar System; it is bigger than the planet Mercury. It is made up of rock and ice. Its surface is quite dark. Io, on the other hand, is a bright orange-yellow. But the most remarkable thing about this moon is that it has active volcanoes. It is the only body in the Solar System, besides the Earth, where volcanoes are now erupting.

The moons that circle farthest from Jupiter are lumps of rock and ice less than 100 kilometres across. Astronomers think that they were once asteroids, which became captured by Jupiter's powerful gravity (see page 48).

The pictures on this page were taken by the US Voyager space probes, which visited the giant planet in 1979. The probes not only took a good look at the moons, they also spotted a faint ring around the planet.

Incredible Io

Io is the most colourful moon in the Solar System, and the most fascinating. The reason is that it has volcanoes that are still erupting. They do not give out molten rock, but molten sulphur. This explains the vivid orange-yellow colouring of the moon.

The Voyager picture above shows one eruption. Material is being shot hundreds of km high. The volcano appears in the map below, which is based on Voyager photographs. It lies in the middle of the 'hoof-print' feature on the left.

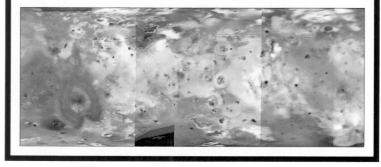

Left Jupiter's narrow ring, pictured by Voyager 2. It runs round the planet's equator. Its discovery came as a great surprise. It is much too faint to be seen from the Earth.

Below A close-up of the surface of Ganymede. The light, grooved regions are quite young features. The bright spots show where meteorites have hit the surface recently and exposed fresh ice.

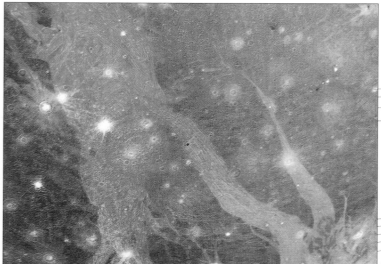

Below The four largest of
Jupiter's moons, compared in size
with the Earth and its Moon. The
pioneering astronomer Galileo
spotted them first, and they are
called the Galilean moons. Their
sizes are as follows:

1 Europa   3,126 km
2 Io   3,632 km
3 Callisto 4,820 km
4 Ganymede 5,276 km

Moon

1

Earth

2

3

4

Voyager to Jupiter

The Voyager probes set out
from Earth in 1977 and
reached Jupiter in 1979.
Voyager 1 got closest
(280,000 km) to the planet.
Voyager 1 sent back the
moon images put together
in the picture above. Going
clockwise from Jupiter, the
moons are Callisto,
Ganymede, Europa and Io.

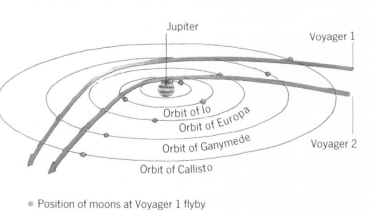

Jupiter

Voyager 1

Orbit of Io
Orbit of Europa
Orbit of Ganymede

Voyager 2

Orbit of Callisto

● Position of moons at Voyager 1 flyby
● Position of moons at Voyager 2 flyby

The moons of Jupiter orbit
in groups. The Galilean moons
form part of the inner group,
going out to about 2 million km.
The middle group orbits 11–12
million km out; and the outer
group, 20–24 million km out. The
moons in the outer group have a
retrograde orbit, meaning that
they circle in the opposite
direction from the others.

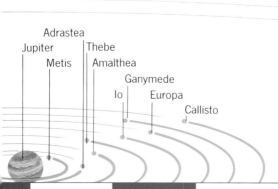

Adrastea
Jupiter   Thebe
  Metis   Amalthea
       Io   Ganymede
            Europa
              Callisto

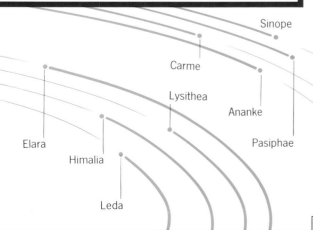

Sinope

Carme

Lysithea

Ananke

Elara

Pasiphae

Himalia

Leda

SATURN: THE RINGED PLANET

Saturn is the second largest planet. It lies twice as far away from the Sun as Jupiter, and therefore appears much dimmer in the night sky. It was the most distant planet known to ancient astronomers.

Seen through a telescope, however, Saturn is the most beautiful planet of all because it is surrounded by flat shining rings. The Italian astronomer Galileo first saw the rings in 1610, and noted that Saturn had 'ears'. We see the rings from different angles year by year as the planet moves in its orbit around the Sun.

Saturn is a great ball of gas and liquid gas, with a cloudy atmosphere. For its size, Saturn is a light planet: it would float in water!

The clouds form into bands in Saturn's atmosphere as the planet spins rapidly on its axis. But the bands are not as obvious as they are on Jupiter. Winds blow furiously in the atmosphere, reaching speeds of up to 1,800 kilometres an hour. They cause great hurricanes to rage all across the planet.

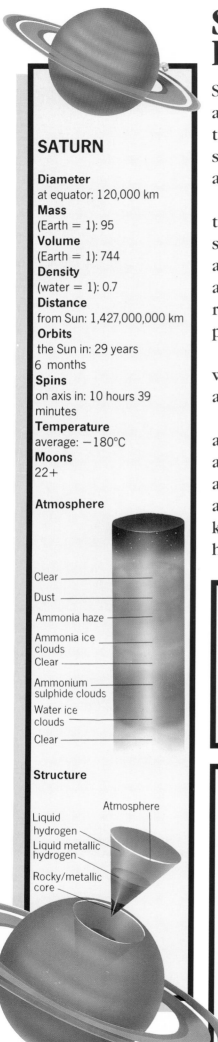

SATURN

Diameter
at equator: 120,000 km
Mass
(Earth = 1): 95
Volume
(Earth = 1): 744
Density
(water = 1): 0.7
Distance
from Sun: 1,427,000,000 km
Orbits
the Sun in: 29 years
6 months
Spins
on axis in: 10 hours 39 minutes
Temperature
average: −180°C
Moons
22+

Atmosphere

Clear
Dust
Ammonia haze
Ammonia ice clouds
Clear
Ammonium sulphide clouds
Water ice clouds
Clear

Structure

Atmosphere
Liquid hydrogen
Liquid metallic hydrogen
Rocky/metallic core

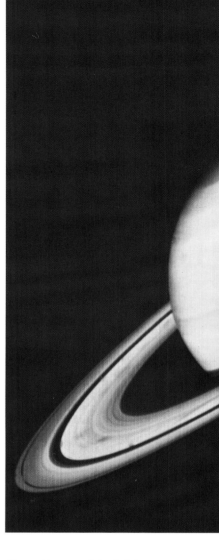

Above Voyager 2 took this picture of Saturn from about 34 million km away. It shows faint belts and zones in the atmosphere, and dark 'spokes' in the rings. Two moons are visible: Dione at the top and Rhea at the bottom.

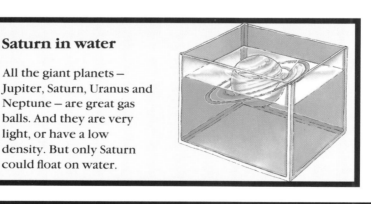

Saturn in water

All the giant planets — Jupiter, Saturn, Uranus and Neptune — are great gas balls. And they are very light, or have a low density. But only Saturn could float on water.

Belts, zones and rings

In a telescope we can see light and dark bands of clouds in Saturn's thick atmosphere, but they are not very clear. We call the dark ones belts and the light ones zones. We can also see three bright shining rings: A, B and C. (Space probes have spied many more rings.) From one side to the other, the rings are about 270,000 km across, or about twice the planet's width.

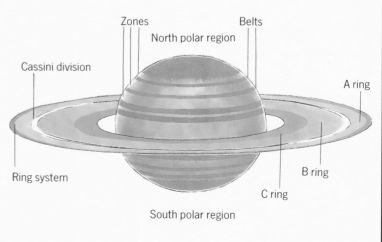

Zones
Belts
North polar region
Cassini division
A ring
Ring system
B ring
C ring
South polar region

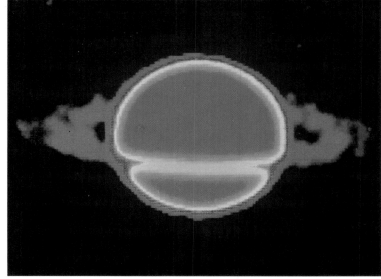

Above Saturn acts like a radio transmitter. The radio waves it gives out can be detected and used to produce a picture like this. Even the rings give off faint waves (blue).

Below Using a computer, NASA scientists produced this Voyager 2 picture of Saturn in false colour. Notice the oval shapes beneath the yellow band. They are great storms. The moons are Dione (top) and Enceladus.

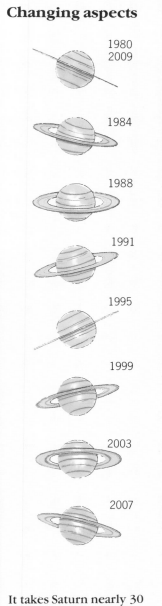

Changing aspects

1980
2009

1984

1988

1991

1995

1999

2003

2007

It takes Saturn nearly 30 years to travel around the Sun. From Earth, we see different views of the rings during this time. These diagrams show the views in different years. In 1995, the rings will be edge-on and almost invisible.

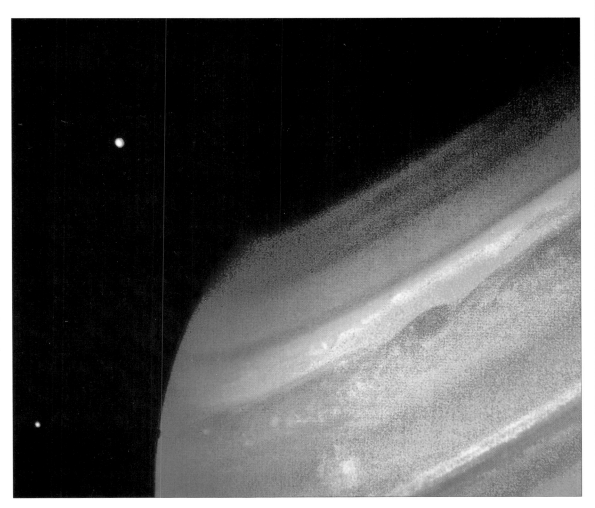

SATURN: RINGS AND MOONS

From the Earth through a telescope, we can see three rings around Saturn. The outer ring (A) is separated from the middle ring (B) by a dark gap. It is called the Cassini division after the Italian astronomer who first spotted it. The B ring is brighter than the A ring, which is much brighter than the inner ring (C).

The Voyager space probes spied many more rings when they visited Saturn in the early 1980s. They discovered that each ring is made up of hundreds of little ringlets. The rings and ringlets are not solid, like hoops. They are rings of light reflected from rocks zooming around the planet at high speed.

Some rings have small moons orbiting on either side. We call them shepherd moons, because they appear to keep the rocks in the rings in place, rather like a shepherd herds a flock of sheep.

The shepherd moons are among 12 new moons discovered by the Voyager probes. With the 10 moons we can see through a telescope, this makes 22 moons in all. Saturn has more moons than any other planet. The largest, Titan, is the second-largest moon in the Solar System, only slightly smaller than Jupiter's Ganymede. It is the only moon that has a thick atmosphere.

Left The rings of Saturn are made up of ringlets numbered in their thousands. This Voyager 2 picture has been printed in false colour to bring out differences in the particles forming the ringlets. The particles in the inner C ring and the Cassini division show up blue. The particles in the B ring change from orange to green, going outwards. The particles in the outer A ring all seem to be similar.

Voyager to Saturn

Voyager 1 and 2 encountered Jupiter in March and July 1979, respectively. Both used Jupiter's gravity to gain speed and shoot them towards Saturn. Voyager 1 made its closest approach in November 1980, Voyager 2 in August 1981. Voyager 1 took this beautiful picture of the rings, before it disappeared into the depths of the Solar System.

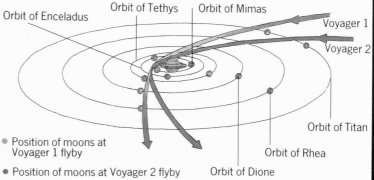

Orbit of Enceladus
Orbit of Tethys
Orbit of Mimas
Voyager 1
Voyager 2
Orbit of Titan
Orbit of Rhea
Orbit of Dione

● Position of moons at Voyager 1 flyby
● Position of moons at Voyager 2 flyby

Left This montage of Voyager photographs shows Saturn with its seven largest moons. Going clockwise from the top right, the moons are: Titan, Iapetus, Tethys, Mimas, Enceladus, Dione and Rhea. The biggest by far is Titan, which is 5,150 km across.

Below Gold-coloured Iapetus measures about 1,440 km across. Curiously, part of its surface is bright, part is dark.

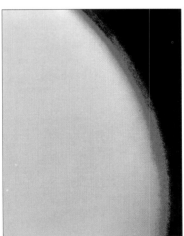

Above The limb of Titan, showing a layer of haze. This moon's atmosphere is thicker than the Earth's and is made up of nitrogen and methane.

Below The orbits of the main moons of Saturn. The largest number circle quite close, out to about 500,000 km. Titan and Hyperion orbit more than twice as far away. Iapetus and Phoebe orbit very much farther out at over 3,500,000 km and nearly 13,000,000 km away, respectively. Phoebe has a backwards orbit.

Iapetus

Titan

Hyperion

Dione

Mimas

Tethys

Enceladus

Janus

Rhea

Phoebe

URANUS, THE TOPSY-TURVY PLANET

Ancient astronomers didn't know there were any planets farther away than Saturn. But in 1781 an English astronomer called William Herschel found one. It was named Uranus. It lies twice as far away as Saturn, and takes 84 Earth-years to circle around the Sun.

Like all the planets, Uranus spins on its axis. Most planets spin nearly in the upright position as they travel in their orbits. But Uranus is tipped right over on its side as it travels. That's why we call it the 'topsy-turvy' planet.

Uranus is made up of gas and liquid gas, like Jupiter and Saturn, but it is smaller. We can't spot it with the naked eye, but we can see it through a telescope. It is pale bluish-green in colour. Like Jupiter and Saturn too, Uranus has a system of rings around it, although they are much too faint to be seen from Earth, even through a telescope.

We can, however, see the five largest of the 15 or more moons that circle around the planet. The most interesting one is Miranda. The Voyager space probes have shown that it looks like no other body in the Solar System. Astronomers think that long ago it was smashed into pieces when it collided with a big asteroid (see page 48). Then the pieces came together again to create the peculiar landscape we see now.

Above No features show up on Uranus. Its bluish-green colour comes from methane gas in its atmosphere.

A new planet

On the night of March 13, 1781, in Bath, England, William Herschel (right) was observing the stars in the constellation Gemini. He was a musician by profession and a keen amateur astronomer.

He spied in his telescope an object that he knew wasn't a star because it showed up as a disc rather than a point of light. He looked at it on the following nights.

When the orbit of the object was calculated, it became clear that Herschel had found a new planet. It was twice as far away from the Sun as Saturn, until then thought to be the most distant planet. The new planet was called Uranus.

Moons and rings

From the Earth we can only spot five moons of Uranus. In order of distance from the planet, they are Miranda, Ariel, Umbriel, Titania and Oberon. They are named after characters in English literature.

Voyager 2 took close-up pictures of these moons. It appears that they are made up of a mixture of rock and water ice. The probe also discovered ten new small moons. It also showed that there are at least ten rings around the planet. They are made up of fast-moving chunks of dark rock.

The two smallest moons are only about 40–50 km across. They circle on either side of the outer ring and probably help keep the ring particles in place. They are another example of shepherd moons (see page 42).

Right A picture of Uranus and its five large moons, taken from Earth with a special electronic camera. It shows the planet and the moons as little 'bumps'. It also shows the ring system around the planet, which we can't normally see.

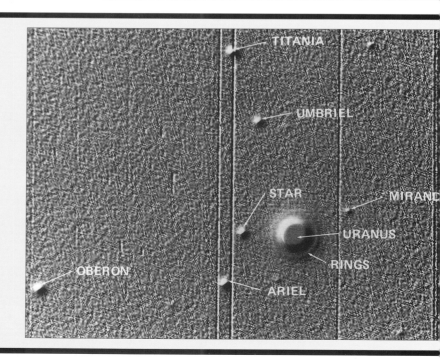

A Voyager bullseye

Voyager 2 left Saturn in August 1981, and spent the next four-and-a-half years travelling to Uranus. It skimmed past the planet on 24 January 1986.

As Voyager approached Uranus, the rings and the orbits of the moons faced it, rather like a target. And Voyager was right on target when it arrived. It had travelled over 5,000 million km since leaving Earth over nine years before. Yet it reached Uranus one minute ahead of schedule!

Scientists worked out that getting Voyager close to Uranus was like sinking a golf putt from a distance of 2,500 km!

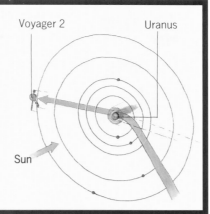

Voyager 2   Uranus

Sun

URANUS

Diameter
at equator: 51,800 km
Mass
(Earth = 1): 14.5
Volume
(Earth = 1): 67
Density
(water = 1): 1.3
Distance
from Sun: 2,869,600,000 km
Orbits
the Sun in: 84 years
Spins
on axis in: 17 hours 14 minutes
Temperature
average: −214°C
Moons
15+

Atmosphere

Hydrogen/
helium/
methane gas

Right This is the view of Uranus you would see if you were orbiting Miranda in a spaceship. The giant planet lies 130,000 km away but still looks vast. How smooth the planet looks compared with the surface of Miranda (below). The moon has great cliffs and mountains and is peppered with craters.

Structure

Atmosphere

Water/ammonia ocean

Rocky/iron core

Right Several deep valleys scar the surface of Ariel. This moon has a diameter of about 1,150 km

Below A close-up of the unique landscape on Miranda, which shows mysterious grooves.

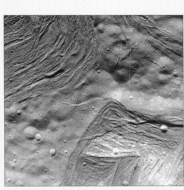

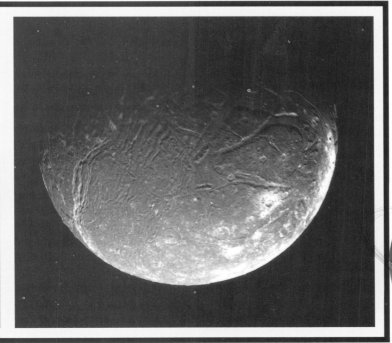

NEPTUNE

After the discovery of Uranus, astronomers began looking for other planets even farther away. And in 1846 a German astronomer named Johann Galle found one, which was called Neptune. The planet is about the same size as Uranus and, through a telescope, appears bluish in colour.

When the Voyager 2 probe flew past Neptune in 1989, it confirmed that the planet is blue. It also spied dark spots and wisps of white cloud in the atmosphere. The dark spots are thought to be great storms, rather like Jupiter's Great Red Spot.

Like the other giant planets, Neptune is a great gas ball. It also has a system of rings around its equator. It has at least eight moons, but we can see only two, Nereid and Triton, from the Earth. Triton is a pinkish world covered with frozen gases. It has a temperature of −236°C, and is the coldest place we know in the Solar System.

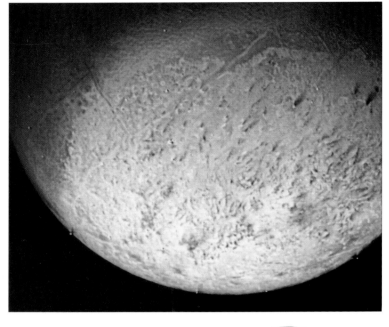

Above The south pole of Triton is covered with a pinkish 'snow' of frozen nitrogen and methane.

Below This Voyager picture of Neptune shows a dark storm centre, called the Great Dark Spot. Strands of white cloud bubble up around the Spot and elsewhere in the thick atmosphere.

Right Neptune and its two main moons (arrowed), photographed from Earth. Triton circles in a backward orbit about 350,000 km out. It is about 2,700 km across, six times the size of Nereid. This orbits up to 9,500,000 km away.

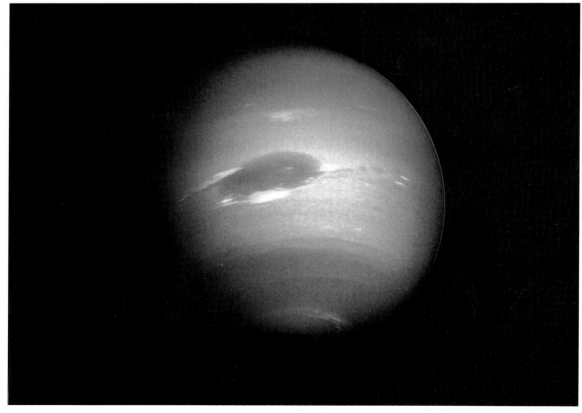

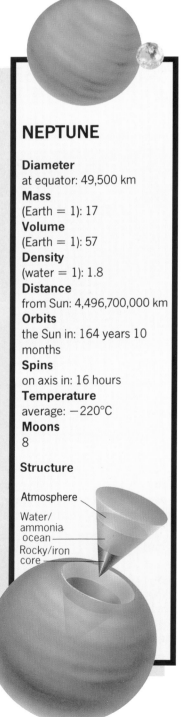

NEPTUNE

Diameter
at equator: 49,500 km
Mass
(Earth = 1): 17
Volume
(Earth = 1): 57
Density
(water = 1): 1.8
Distance
from Sun: 4,496,700,000 km
Orbits
the Sun in: 164 years 10 months
Spins
on axis in: 16 hours
Temperature
average: −220°C
Moons
8

Structure

Atmosphere

Water/ammonia ocean

Rocky/iron core

PLUTO

The search for still more planets continued into the present century. In 1930 an American astronomer named Clyde Tombaugh was successful. He spotted a tiny moving 'star', which proved to be a ninth planet, Pluto. It lies so far away that it takes nearly 250 Earth-years to circle around the Sun. At the moment Pluto is not the most distant planet. It is circling inside Neptune's orbit (until 1999).

We know little about Pluto. It is so distant that it appears only as a speck in telescopes. And no space probes have visited it yet.

Pluto is a very tiny world, and is by far the smallest planet. It is much smaller even than our Moon. It has a moon of its own, called Charon. Surprisingly, Charon is half as big across as Pluto. This is why astronomers often call Pluto-Charon a double planet.

Above The first clear picture of Pluto and Charon, taken by the Hubble Space Telescope in 1990.

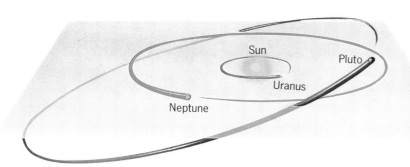

Above Pluto's orbit takes it a long way above and below the orbits of the other planets. At times Pluto travels as far as 7,000,000,000 km from the Sun.

Planet X

Some astronomers do not think Pluto is the last planet. It cannot cause the wobbles in the orbits of Uranus and Neptune because its gravity is too low.

They reckon that there must therefore be a tenth planet, Planet X. It must lie a very long way away, otherwise it would have been discovered already. And it must be large — to cause the disturbances in the orbits.

PLUTO

Diameter
at equator: 2,284 km
Mass
(Earth = 1): 0.002 (1/500)
Volume
(Earth = 1): 0.005 (1/200)
Density
(water = 1): 2
Distance
from Sun: 5,900,000,000 km
Orbits
the Sun in: 247 years 8 months
Spins
on axis in: 6 days 9 hours
Temperature
average: −230°C
Moons
1

Structure

Water/methane ice

Rocky core?

The Planet hunters

After the discovery of Uranus in 1781 and Neptune in 1846, astronomers found that their orbits were not quite right. This made them think there must be a ninth planet.

In the early 1900s, the American astronomer Percival Lowell, worked out where he thought the new planet should be: somewhere in the constellations Gemini or Taurus. He started looking for it, but in vain. He died in 1916.

A young astronomer

named Clyde Tombaugh eventually continued Lowell's work at his observatory in Flagstaff Arizona. He began searching for the new planet in 1927.

On February 29, 1930, he

was looking at the two pictures shown below, taken on January 23 and 27. One 'star' had moved. It was no star, but the new planet — Pluto. It was close to where Lowell had said it would be.

ASTEROIDS AND METEOROIDS

The small rocky inner planets, from Mercury to Mars, lie quite close together in space (see **page 10**). From Mars to Jupiter there is quite a gap, where we might expect to find another planet. But instead we find a swarm of much smaller bodies. We call them asteroids or minor planets.

Astronomers know about thousands of these asteroids, but most of them are rocky lumps only a few tens of kilometres across. Even the biggest, Ceres, is only about 1,000 kilometres across. Most of the asteroids circle around the Sun in a broad band that we call the asteroid belt. A few stray farther afield, and sometimes come dangerously close to the Earth.

The Earth is bombarded all the time, however, with tiny rocky particles, which we call meteoroids. These specks are pulled to the Earth by gravity and plunge into the atmosphere at high speed. Friction (rubbing together) with the air particles produces heat and makes them glow red-hot and eventually burn up. At night you can often see the fiery streaks they make in the sky. We call these streaks meteors or shooting stars.

Sometimes a big piece of rock enters the atmosphere and only partly burns up. What is left reaches the ground, and we call it a meteorite. If it is big enough, it can gouge a large hole, or crater, in the ground.

Above Two asteroids (arrowed) appear in this photograph. The camera was following the stars, which appear as points. The asteroids show trails as they move against the background of stars.

Right The asteroid belt lies between about 300 and 500 million km from the Sun. Some of the asteroids that travel outside the asteroid belt are shown here.

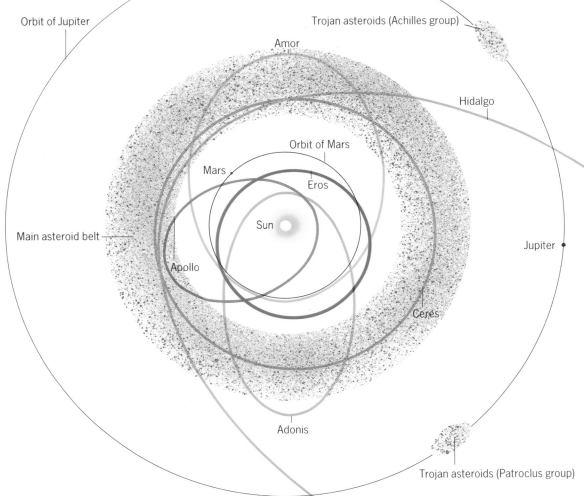

Orbit of Jupiter

Amor

Trojan asteroids (Achilles group)

Hidalgo

Orbit of Mars

Mars

Eros

Sun

Main asteroid belt

Apollo

Jupiter

Ceres

Adonis

Trojan asteroids (Patroclus group)

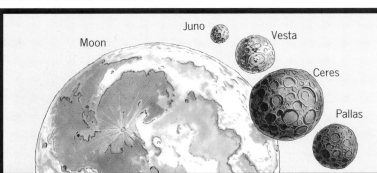

Moon

Juno

Vesta

Ceres

Pallas

The first asteroids

The Italian astronomer Giuseppe Piazzi discovered the first asteroid, Ceres, on January 1, 1801. Pallas was spotted in 1802, Juno in 1804 and Vesta in 1807. These asteroids have diameters of about 1,000, 600, 250 and 540 km respectively.

Since 1845, several more have been found almost every year. The orbits of nearly 3,000 have been calculated. Only about 200 are larger than 100 km in diameter.

Left The famous Meteor Crater in the Arizona Desert, USA. It is the best example of a meteorite crater on Earth. It is about 1,265 m across and 175 m deep. Thanks to the dry desert conditions, it has been well preserved. The meteorite that gouged it out plunged to Earth about 50,000 years ago. It must have weighed at least 100,000 tonnes.

Below A fireball streaks through the night sky. This is the name we give to a large meteoroid particle burning up in the atmosphere. This one was photographed in a meteor shower. Showers take place several times a year, and a hundred or more meteors may be seen every hour.

Bombarding Earth

Every day millions of tiny meteoroids rain down on the Earth from outer space. The smallest burn up in the atmosphere 100 km or more above the ground. They are too faint to be seen in the night sky. The ones we see as meteors (about the size of a grain of sand) burn up at about 80 km high. Large lumps survive and hit the ground as meteorites. Some are stony, others are metallic, made up of iron and nickel.

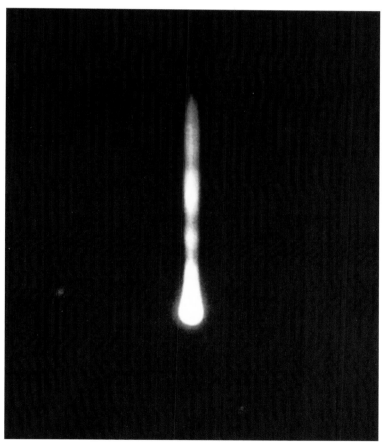

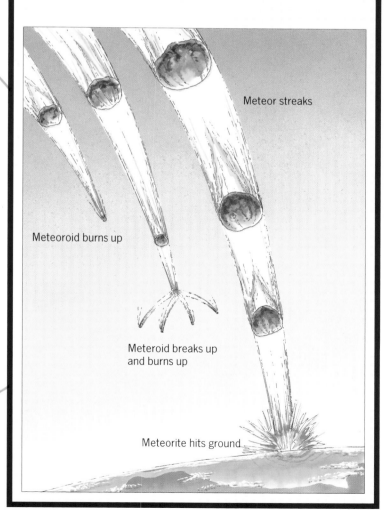

Meteor streaks

Meteoroid burns up

Meteroid breaks up and burns up

Meteorite hits ground

Death to dinosaurs

In the past the Earth has been bombarded by huge meteorites. Scientists have found evidence of this in the rock layers. One such onslaught happened about 65 million years ago. It may have caused such a change in conditions on Earth that many forms of life were wiped out, among them the dinosaurs.

The dinosaur *Brachiosaurus*

COMETS

We can see meteors and one or more of the planets on most nights of the year. But sometimes we receive more spectacular visitors to our skies, called comets. At their brightest, these bodies outshine the stars. Some of them grow long tails that stretch halfway across the heavens.

Ancient peoples used to fear comets because they appeared suddenly and could not be explained. We know now that comets are lumps of rock, ice and dust that travel in towards the Sun from far out in the Solar System. As a comet gets near the Sun, the ice melts and turns to vapour (gas). The dust is set free. The gas and dust form a cloud that reflects the Sun's light, and the comet becomes visible.

Most comets appear in the skies without warning. But a few return at regular intervals. We call these periodic comets. The most famous is Halley's comet, which returns to our skies every 75 years or so. It last appeared in 1986, and will be seen again in the year 2061.

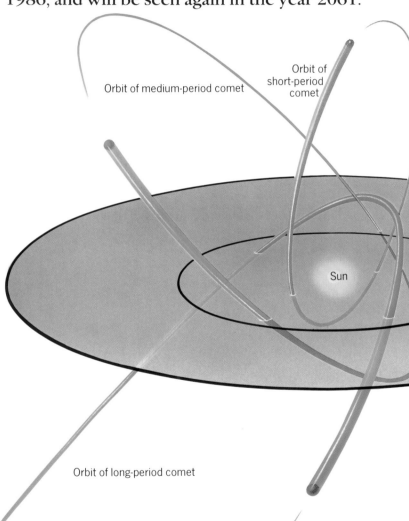

Orbit of medium-period comet

Orbit of short-period comet

Sun

Orbit of long-period comet

Above Comet Ikeya-Seki in the dawn sky. It was the brightest comet of 1965, and was visible in broad daylight in some parts of the world. It will not be seen again until the year 2845.

Right Short-period comets lap the Sun in just a few years. Medium-period comets take decades, and long-period ones centuries. It is impossible to predict when, or even if, some comets will return.

A bad omen

The year 1066 was a bad one for the English. They were defeated at the Battle of Hastings and their King, Harold, was killed. They blamed it all on a bright comet that had appeared in the skies that year.

It appears in the famous Bayeux Tapestry, which commemorates the Battle of Hastings. The picture on the right shows Harold's courtiers trembling with fear at the comet.

In 1682, the English Astronomer Royal Edmond Halley saw a comet, and calculated the orbit. He found it was similar to the orbits of comets seen in 1531 and 1607. So he suggested they were all the same comet. He predicted it would return in 1758. It did. It has since been called Halley's Comet. Records show that it was spotted as early as 240 B.C.

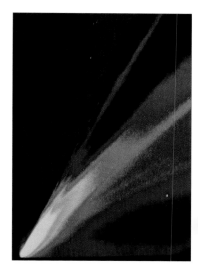

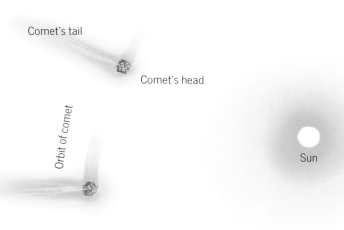

Comet's tail

Comet's head

Orbit of comet

Sun

Tail changes direction

Below As comets head towards the Sun, they start to melt. A cloud of gas and dust forms around them. The solar wind forces it into a tail. More gas and dust is released, and the tail grows. As the comet loops around the Sun, the tail changes direction, always pointing away from the Sun. As the comet travels away, it gradually freezes up and its tail grows smaller and smaller.

Above Comet West of 1976. The photograph has been printed in false colour to bring out differences in brightness. Comet West was one of the brightest comets this century, but it will not return to Earth's skies for hundreds of thousands of years.

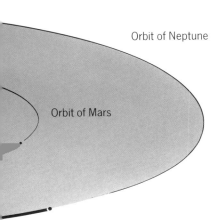

Orbit of Neptune

Orbit of Mars

Right Halley's Comet, photographed from Australia in mid-March 1986. It shows a well-developed tail. Disappointingly, the comet was not as bright that year as it had been on its last visit, in 1910.

The heart of Halley

No comet has been better studied than Halley's. In 1985 five space probes set off from Earth to spy on the comet from close-quarters: two Russian, two Japanese and one European.

The one that got closest was Europe's Giotto. Launched in July 1985, it reached Halley in March 1986. It sent back spectacular pictures like the one on the right, which was taken from about 18,000 km away. It shows two bright jets of gas erupting from the nucleus, or heart, of the comet. This appears to be potato-shaped, and measures about 15 km long and 8 km across.

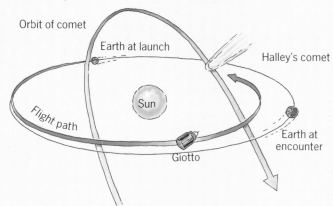

Orbit of comet

Earth at launch

Sun

Flight path

Giotto

Halley's comet

Earth at encounter

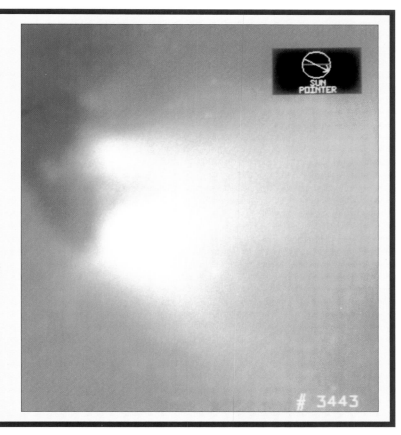

Whirling above our heads like a great celestial carousel, the night sky is ablaze with stars by the million. The patterns of bright stars, which we call constellations, stay the same century after century. They enable us to find our way through the stellar maze.

THE WHIRLING HEAVENS

Every morning the Sun rises in the east. The sky lightens and it becomes daytime. During the day the Sun moves across the sky and sets in the west. The sky darkens and it becomes night-time. The next morning the Sun rises again. It seems to have made a complete circle around the Earth in 24 hours, travelling from east to west.

But this is not what has happened. In fact, the Sun has stood still and it is the Earth that has moved. It has spun round in space like a top, from west to east. It is daytime at a place when it spins into the sunlight. It is night-time at a place when it spins out of the sunlight into the darkness of the Earth's shadow.

Even on a moonless night, the sky is not completely dark, for it is lit up by thousands upon thousands of twinkling stars. They look like so many sparkling jewels set in a velvet backcloth.

If you stare at the night sky for any length of time, you notice that the stars seem to wheel round overhead. But this movement is again caused by the Earth spinning round; the stars in fact stay still.

The ancient astronomers believed that the Earth was the centre of the universe. It was fixed, they said, in the middle of a great dark globe, which was spinning round and round, and that the stars were stuck on the inside of this globe. They called it the celestial sphere.

We now know that there is no rotating celestial sphere. But the idea is very useful in astronomy. It helps us pinpoint the positions of the stars in the sky.

Above Star trails in the northern sky, in the Northern Hemisphere. The stars make these trails as they appear to circle the heavens. A star near the centre has hardly moved at all. It is Polaris, also called the North Star and the Pole Star. It hardly moves because it is almost directly above the North Pole, in line with the Earth's axis. Notice how the colours of the stars show up.

The planetarium

In the picture, the Moon and a starry sky appear on the domed roof of a planetarium. The images are put there by a very complicated projector, shaped like a dumb-bell.

The planetarium projector is made up of some 30,000 parts. It can show the night sky for any latitude and for any time in the present, past and even the future.

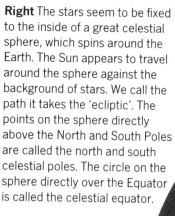

Right The stars seem to be fixed to the inside of a great celestial sphere, which spins around the Earth. The Sun appears to travel around the sphere against the background of stars. We call the path it takes the 'ecliptic'. The points on the sphere directly above the North and South Poles are called the north and south celestial poles. The circle on the sphere directly over the Equator is called the celestial equator.

Celestial equator

Sun

Ecliptic

Equator

Earth

Celestial sphere

Near and far

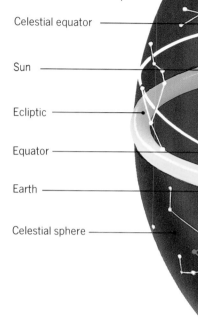

Bright star

Dim star

Apparent brightness in sky

Most stars that appear close together in the night sky are actually a long way apart. They appear close only because they happen to lie in the same direction.

If one star seems brighter than another, we can't say that it actually is brighter. It may be that the brighter-looking star is much closer to us and looks brighter for that reason.

Star maps

Astronomers use the idea of the celestial sphere to draw star maps. The diagram shows how they split the sphere into segments, and then flatten the segments out. This method causes some distortion because it is showing a curved surface on flat paper.

Usually astronomers split the sphere into six segments.

They usually mark two scales on their maps, similar to the latitude and longitude on an ordinary map. They are called declination and right ascension, respectively.

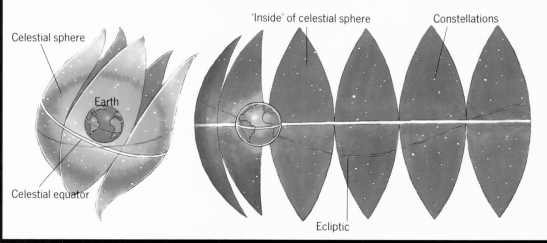

Celestial sphere

Earth

Celestial equator

'Inside' of celestial sphere

Constellations

Ecliptic

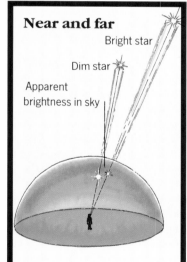

THE CONSTELLATIONS

When you first look up at the night sky, all the stars look much the same and seem to be scattered higgledy-piggledy about. But soon you notice that some stars are brighter than others, and form patterns that you can recognize. If you look in the same part of the sky at about the same time two nights running, you will again see the same star patterns. We call them constellations.

Recognizable star patterns can be found in all parts of the sky, and provide a useful way of finding our way around it. Ancient Greek astronomers over 2,000 years ago saw much the same constellations that we see today and gave them the names we still use. They named them after figures they imagined they could see in the patterns: animals, people and everyday objects. They took these figures from the Greek myths, and made up stories about how the figures got into the sky.

We know the constellations today by the Latin versions of the Greek names and also by English translations of these names. Two familiar animal constellations visible in the Northern Hemisphere of the world are Ursa Major, the Great Bear, and Draco, the Dragon. In the Southern Hemisphere Centaurus, the Centaur, and Scorpius, the Scorpion, are seen easily. Among people depicted are the hunter Orion, and the heroine Andromeda, which can be seen in both hemispheres.

Above Orion (Hunter) is one of the most striking of all the constellations. It lies on the celestial equator and can be seen well in both the Northern and Southern Hemispheres. The diagram outlines the pattern made by the bright stars. Only two have names. The others are given Greek letters. The bright patch below the three stars of Orion's belt is the Orion Nebula.

The planisphere

A planisphere is a device for finding the stars in the night sky. It is made of two discs, one of which rotates over the other.

A star map is drawn on the bottom disc, which has a scale around the edge showing every date of the year. The top disc has an oval window in it, with a scale around the edge marked in hours.

To use it, rotate the top disc until the hour of observation lines up with the date. All the stars visible in the sky now appear in the window. Hold the planisphere above your head, and the sky should match the map.

Signs of the zodiac

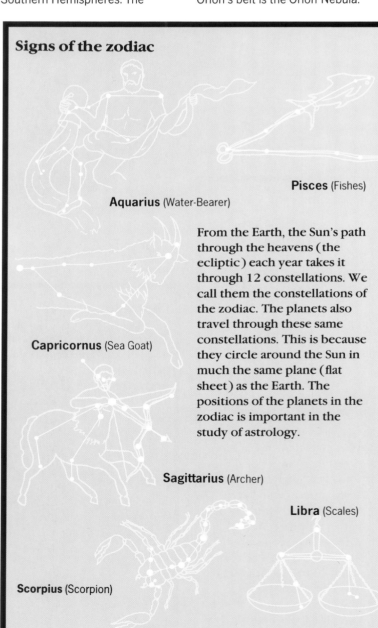

Aquarius (Water-Bearer)

Pisces (Fishes)

Capricornus (Sea Goat)

From the Earth, the Sun's path through the heavens (the ecliptic) each year takes it through 12 constellations. We call them the constellations of the zodiac. The planets also travel through these same constellations. This is because they circle around the Sun in much the same plane (flat sheet) as the Earth. The positions of the planets in the zodiac is important in the study of astrology.

Sagittarius (Archer)

Libra (Scales)

Scorpius (Scorpion)

Above Crux (Southern Cross) is the easiest constellation to recognize in far southern skies. Nearby are the two brightest stars in Centaurus (Centaur), seen on the right in this picture.

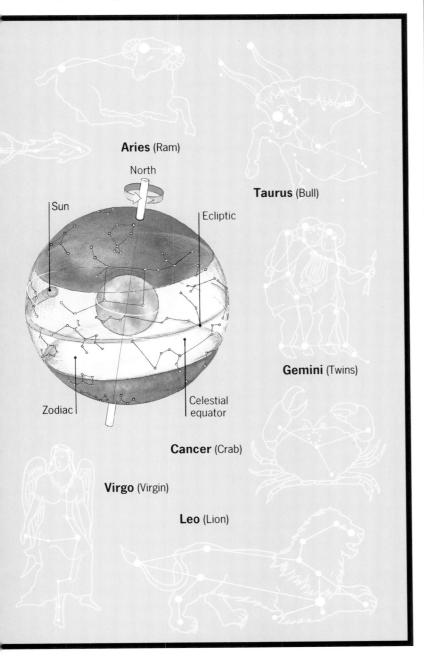

Aries (Ram)

North

Sun

Ecliptic

Taurus (Bull)

Gemini (Twins)

Zodiac

Celestial equator

Cancer (Crab)

Virgo (Virgin)

Leo (Lion)

Viewing the night sky

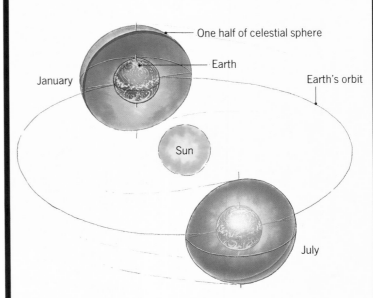

One half of celestial sphere

Earth

January

Earth's orbit

Sun

July

As the Earth revolves round the Sun the night sky is always the part which lies away from the Sun. During the day the Sun obliterates any stars which lie beyond it. In January for example, the brightness of the daytime Sun outshines the constellations of Capricornus (Sea goat) and Aquarius (Water bearer) but they are visible to us at night six months later in July.

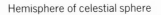

Hemisphere of celestial sphere

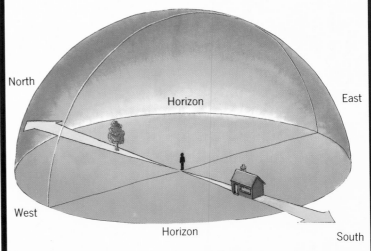

North

Horizon

East

West

Horizon

South

Wherever you are, the night sky appears as a half-sphere overhead, rather like an upturned bowl (above). The 'bowl' appears to sit on the ground. It meets the ground on all sides at the horizon. The constellations you see will depend on which direction you look. In the star maps that follow, we have shown views of the night sky looking north and looking south (below).

The sky looking north

The sky looking south

NORTHERN CONSTELLATIONS

This star map shows all the constellations that appear in the northern half of the celestial sphere. The celestial equator runs around the circumference (outer edge) of the map. Wherever you live in the Northern Hemisphere of the world, you will be able to see all of these constellations at some time.

Which constellations you see on a particular night will depend on several things, including the time of the night and the time of the year. It will depend in which direction you are looking – north, east, south or west. And it will depend on where you are.

You will also be able to see during the year some of the constellations that appear in the southern half of the celestial sphere. These are shown in the map on page 62. The farther south you live, the more southern constellations you will see. And if you live on the Equator, you will see all the constellations at some time during the year.

If you live in northern Europe or North America, you will be able to see some constellations in the northern sky every night of the year. They include Ursa Minor (Little Bear), Ursa Major (Great Bear), Cassiopeia and Cepheus. We call these constellations circumpolar, which means around the pole.

The celestial pole is the point on the celestial sphere directly above the Earth's North Pole. It is marked by the star Polaris, also called the Pole Star or North Star. Polaris appears fixed in the sky, unlike the other stars.

Right Constellations visible in the northern half of the celestial sphere, as far south as the celestial equator. The line of the ecliptic marks the path of the Sun through the northern heavens.

Below The figures the constellations are meant to represent appear in ancient Greek mythology. The tale behind Ursa Major, the Great Bear, is this. A woman named Callisto bore a child of Zeus, king of the Gods. Zeus's wife, Hera, took revenge by turning her into a hairy bear.

Ursa Major

Cygnus

Left An illustration from a Sanskrit (ancient Indian) manuscript, showing constellations. Easy to recognize are Sagittarius (Archer), Capricornus (Sea Goat), Pegasus (Flying Horse) and Andromeda. Another illustration from the same manuscript appears on page 62.

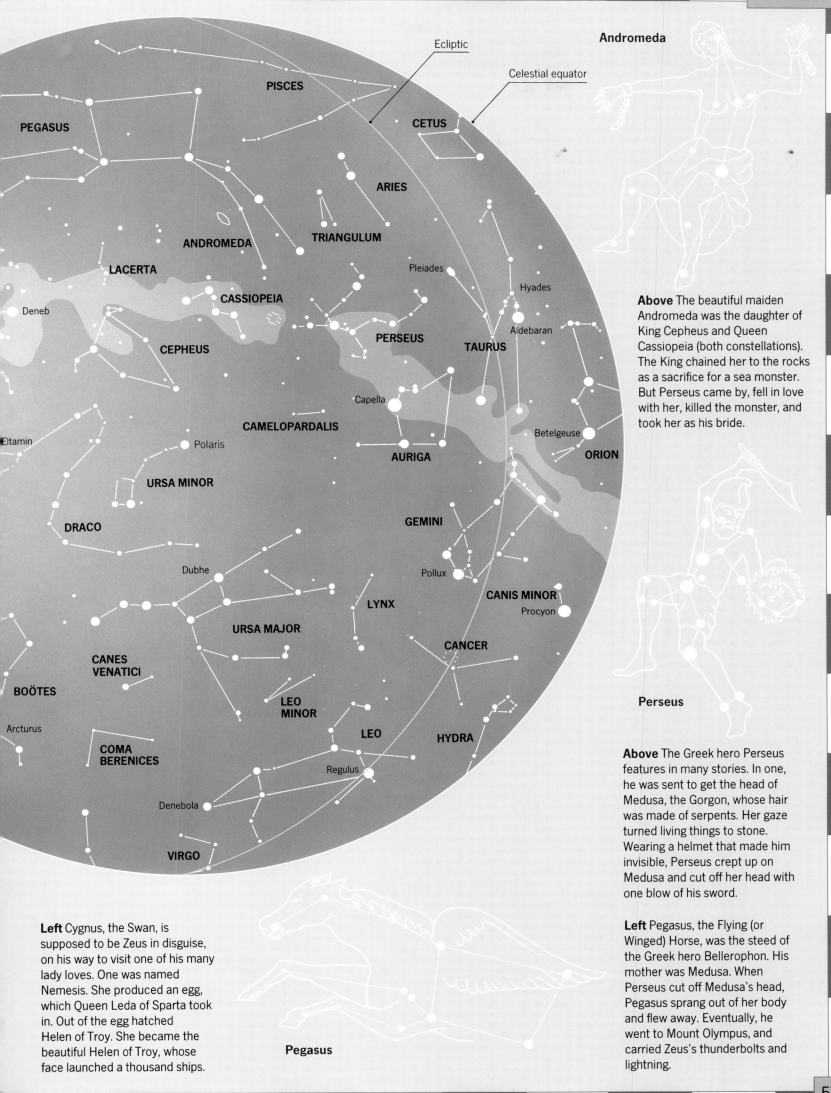

Ecliptic

Celestial equator

PISCES

CETUS

PEGASUS

ARIES

TRIANGULUM

ANDROMEDA

Pleiades

LACERTA

Hyades

Deneb

CASSIOPEIA

PERSEUS

Aldebaran

CEPHEUS

TAURUS

Capella

Eltamin

CAMELOPARDALIS

Polaris

Betelgeuse

AURIGA

ORION

URSA MINOR

GEMINI

DRACO

Dubhe

Pollux

LYNX

CANIS MINOR

Procyon

URSA MAJOR

CANCER

CANES
VENATICI

BOÖTES

LEO
MINOR

Arcturus

LEO

HYDRA

COMA
BERENICES

Regulus

Denebola

VIRGO

Andromeda

Above The beautiful maiden Andromeda was the daughter of King Cepheus and Queen Cassiopeia (both constellations). The King chained her to the rocks as a sacrifice for a sea monster. But Perseus came by, fell in love with her, killed the monster, and took her as his bride.

Perseus

Above The Greek hero Perseus features in many stories. In one, he was sent to get the head of Medusa, the Gorgon, whose hair was made of serpents. Her gaze turned living things to stone. Wearing a helmet that made him invisible, Perseus crept up on Medusa and cut off her head with one blow of his sword.

Left Cygnus, the Swan, is supposed to be Zeus in disguise, on his way to visit one of his many lady loves. One was named Nemesis. She produced an egg, which Queen Leda of Sparta took in. Out of the egg hatched Helen of Troy. She became the beautiful Helen of Troy, whose face launched a thousand ships.

Pegasus

Left Pegasus, the Flying (or Winged) Horse, was the steed of the Greek hero Bellerophon. His mother was Medusa. When Perseus cut off Medusa's head, Pegasus sprang out of her body and flew away. Eventually, he went to Mount Olympus, and carried Zeus's thunderbolts and lightning.

NORTHERN CONSTELLATIONS: WINTER

Looking North

In the north-east is the most familiar star pattern in northern skies, the Plough. It is part of the constellation Ursa Major (Great Bear). The three stars in the handle of the Plough and the four stars of the ploughshare all have about the same brightness. If you look closely at the middle star in the handle, you can see that it has a fainter companion – it is a double star.

Polaris, the Pole Star, is at the tail end of Ursa Minor (Little Bear) but is not easy to spot. So use the two stars at the end of the ploughshare as pointers to direct your eyes to it.

Towards the west is the fuzzy band of the Milky Way, and beyond that the unmistakable square of Pegasus (Flying Horse). High overhead on the edge of the Milky Way is the brightest star in this part of the heavens, Capella in Auriga (Charioteer). Further down within the Milky Way the W-shape of Cassiopeia stands out. Near the horizon is Cygnus (Swan), whose brightest star is Deneb. Cygnus is one of the few constellations that actually looks like the figure it is supposed to represent. It really does look like a flying swan, with outstretched neck and wings. It is also called the Northern Cross.

Above The North American Nebula in Cygnus. This bright cloud of glowing gas is well named, because it does have a similar shape to the continent of North America. The darker areas in the picture show where dust clouds have blocked light coming from behind.

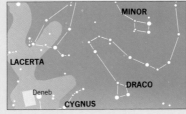

Right Constellations observers in North America and Europe would see at about 10.30 pm in mid-January, looking north.

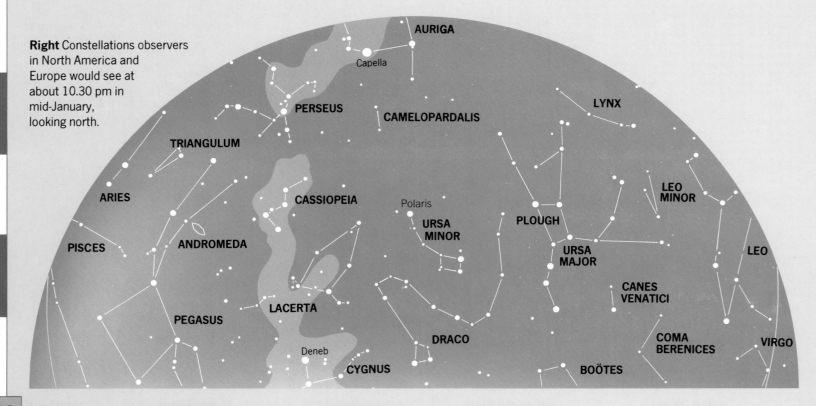

Looking South

It is in southern skies in the Northern Hemisphere that the greatest changes can be observed in the night sky season by season.

The large bright constellation of Orion, seen here west of the Milky Way, dominates the winter sky. Its two brightest stars are the reddish supergiant Betelgeuse and the brilliant white Rigel. Beneath the three stars that make up Orion's belt, is the bright glow of the Orion Nebula. Seen through a telescope, this nebula is one of the most magnificent sights in the whole heavens.

West of Orion and slightly higher in the sky is Taurus (Bull). This constellation has only one really bright star, the reddish Aldebaran. But it is interesting because it contains two open star clusters, the Hyades and the Pleiades, or Seven Sisters. The Pleiades is easily seen with the naked eye, and looks really beautiful through binoculars.

If you trace an imaginary line from Aldebaran, through Orion's belt to the edge of the Milky Way, you will come to the brightest star in the whole heavens – Sirius. This blue-white star, in Canis Major (Great Dog), is often called the Dog Star.

Right The Pleiades star cluster in Taurus. It is also called the Seven Sisters because if you have very good eyesight, you should be able to see its seven brightest stars. An amateur astronomer took this picture with a fast film, using an exposure time of five minutes.

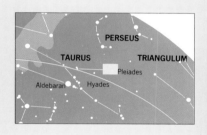

Right Constellations observers in North America and Europe would see at about 10.30 pm in mid-January, looking south.

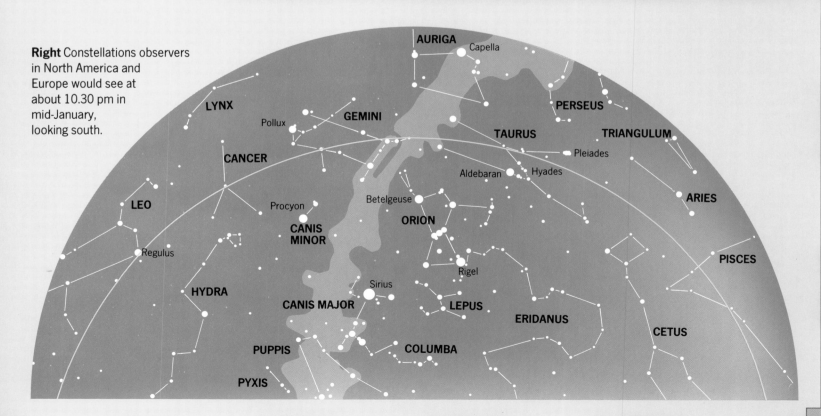

NORTHERN CONSTELLATIONS: SUMMER

Looking North

This map shows a northerly view of the heavens six months after the map on page 58. The constellations have moved through a half-circle.

Curving its 'tail' around Ursa Minor (Little Bear) and thrusting its 'head' up to the zenith (highest point) is the long winding Draco (Dragon). The Plough now lies in the north-west. Lower down near the western horizon is the easily recognizable shape of Leo (Lion).

The region between Leo, Virgo (Virgin) and Coma Berenices (Berenice's Hair) has few bright stars. But powerful telescopes show it to be exceptionally rich in galaxies. In fact the galaxies cluster together in their hundreds.

The Milky Way now lies in the north-east, with the bright Capella in Auriga (Charioteer) near the horizon, and Deneb in Cygnus (Swan) high up. Pegasus (Flying Horse) now lies in the east. It is linked with Andromeda.

Andromeda is not a prominent constellation, but it is interesting because it contains a fuzzy patch we call the Andromeda Nebula. You can easily see this with the naked eye near the edge of the Milky Way, to the right and a little below the 'W' of Cassiopeia. It is not a nebula, however, but a separate galaxy over two million light-years away. It is the farthest object we can see with the naked eye.

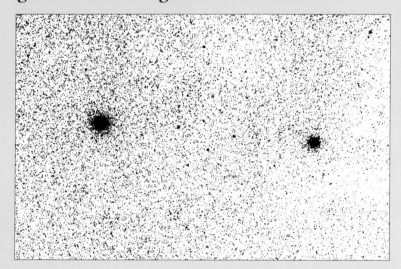

Left The Double Cluster in Perseus, also called the Sword Handle. It is a pair of open star clusters. This picture is printed as a negative. Astronomers often do this to bring out extra detail in a picture.

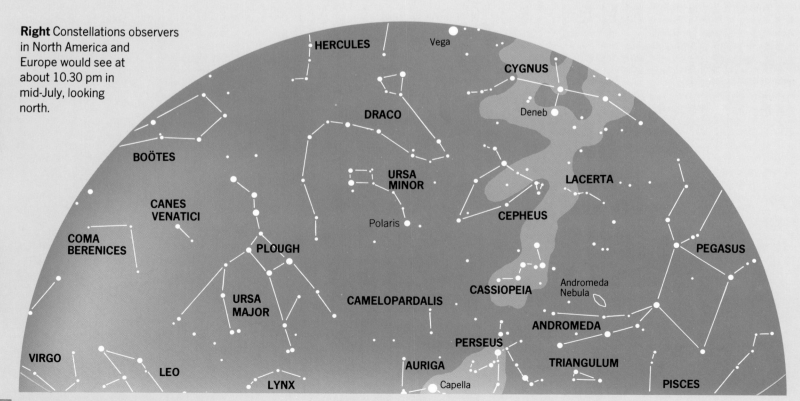

Right Constellations observers in North America and Europe would see at about 10.30 pm in mid-July, looking north.

Looking South

The Milky Way cuts across the middle of the sky and passes through some of the most interesting constellations in the summer sky. Due south, just above the horizon, is Scorpius (Scorpion). It is well-named: bright stars outline a scorpion-like figure with a curved tail at one end and branching claws at the other. The brightest star at the head is Antares, a red supergiant. It is one of the biggest stars we can see, hundreds of times bigger than the Sun.

Just above Scorpius within the Milky Way is Sagittarius (Archer), whose 'bow' is outlined by bright stars. This part of the Milky Way is particularly bright. Through binoculars it looks magnificent, with stars seemingly packed together in their hundreds of thousands. They appear like this because you are looking towards the centre of our Galaxy.

Further along the Milky Way lies Aquila (Eagle), whose brightest star is Altair. If you look overhead, you will see that Altair forms one corner of a triangle of bright stars. The other two are Deneb in Cygnus (Swan) and Vega in Lyra (Lyre). This trio of bright stars forms what is called the Summer Triangle.

Also high overhead is Hercules. This constellation contains a fine globular cluster (M13), almost visible to the naked eye.

Above The beautiful Lagoon Nebula in Sagittarius, just visible to the naked eye. It has a dark 'dust lane' through the middle, blocking its light. There are several other nebulae in Sagittarius, making it one of the most spectacular of all the constellations.

Right Constellations observers in North America and Europe would see at about 10.30 pm in mid-July, looking south.

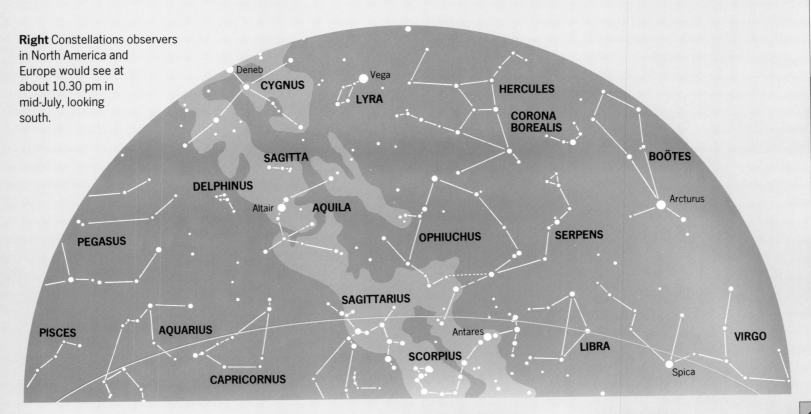

SOUTHERN CONSTELLATIONS

This star map shows all the constellations in the southern half of the celestial sphere. The celestial equator runs around the circumference (outer edge) of the map.

Wherever you live in the Southern Hemisphere, you will be able to see all of these constellations at some time during the year. Which ones you see on a particular night will depend on the time, the season, and in which direction you are looking. It will also depend on where you are.

You will also be able to see some constellations of the northern half of the celestial sphere. These are shown on pages 58–61. If you live on the Equator, you will be able to see every constellation there is at some time during the year.

Looking south in the Southern Hemisphere, some constellations are circumpolar and are always visible. They include Crux (Southern Cross), the most famous of all southern constellations, Carina (Keel), Musca (Fly), Pavo (Peacock) and Triangulum Australe (Southern Triangle). Also circumpolar are the Large and Small Magellanic Clouds, which are nearby galaxies. The longest arm of Crux points in the direction of the south celestial pole. But there is no pole star in southern skies as there is in the north.

Below This picture includes zodiac constellations, Centaurus (Centaur), Hydra (Water-Snake) and Ophiuchus (Serpent-Bearer).

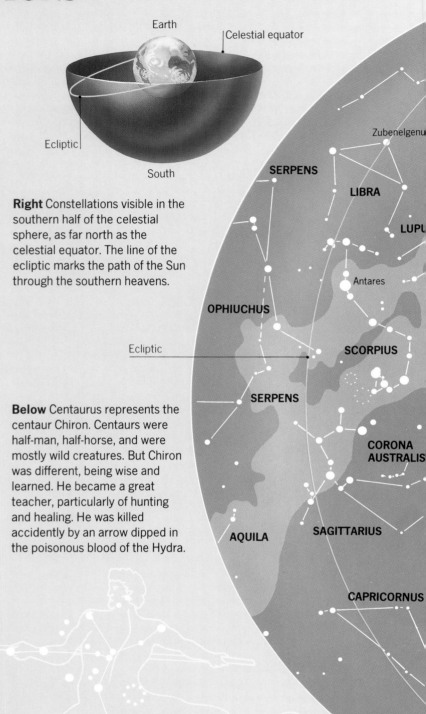

Right Constellations visible in the southern half of the celestial sphere, as far north as the celestial equator. The line of the ecliptic marks the path of the Sun through the southern heavens.

Below Centaurus represents the centaur Chiron. Centaurs were half-man, half-horse, and were mostly wild creatures. But Chiron was different, being wise and learned. He became a great teacher, particularly of hunting and healing. He was killed accidently by an arrow dipped in the poisonous blood of the Hydra.

Centaurus

Right Hydra, the Water-Snake, is the largest constellation. In myth it was a monster with many heads. One of the labours of the hero Hercules was to kill the Hydra, but this proved difficult as soon as he cut off one head, another two grew in its place. Hercules won in the end, and tipped his arrows with the Hydra's poisonous blood.

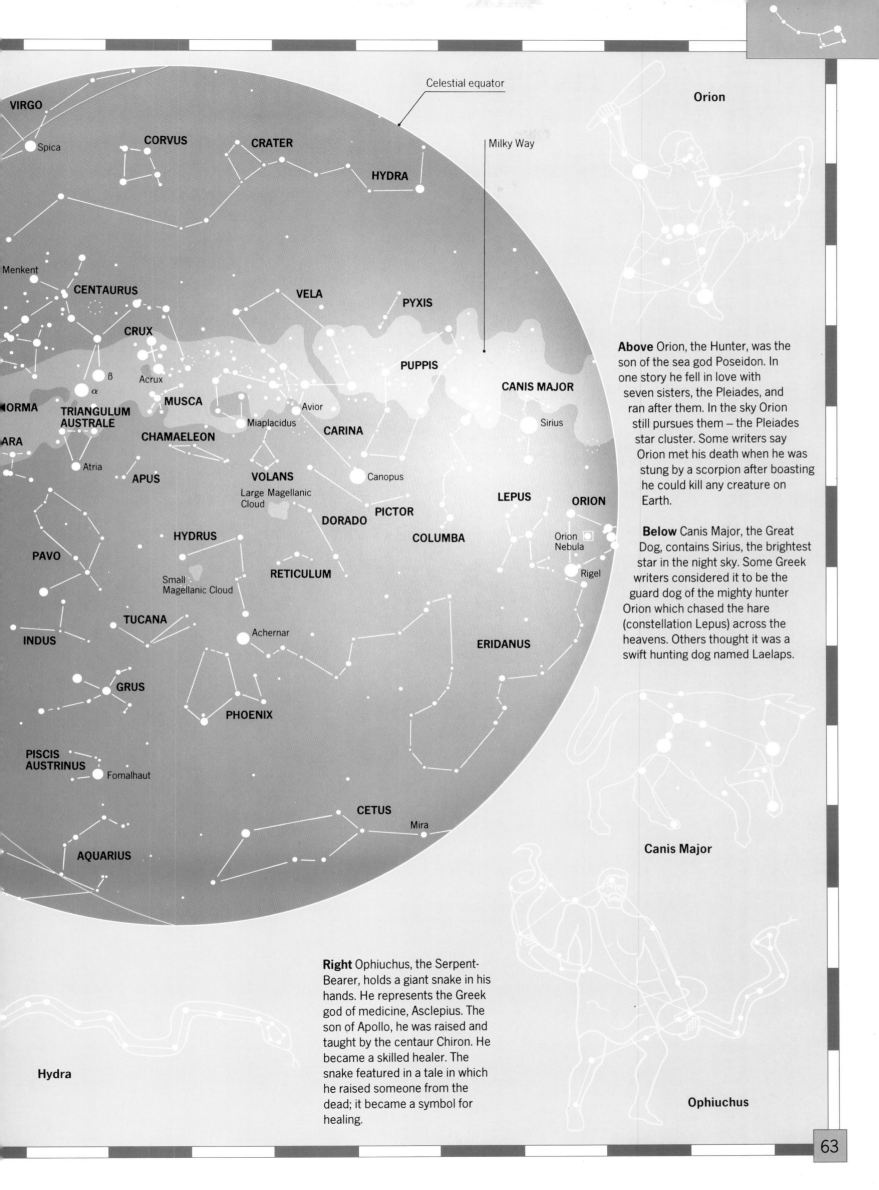

Celestial equator

Milky Way

VIRGO

Spica

CORVUS

CRATER

HYDRA

Menkent

CENTAURUS

CRUX

β

Acrux

α

NORMA

TRIANGULUM
AUSTRALE

MUSCA

ARA

CHAMAELEON

Atria

APUS

VELA

PYXIS

PUPPIS

CANIS MAJOR

Avior

Sirius

Miaplacidus

CARINA

VOLANS

Canopus

Large Magellanic
Cloud

DORADO

PICTOR

LEPUS

ORION

PAVO

HYDRUS

COLUMBA

Orion
Nebula

Small
Magellanic Cloud

RETICULUM

Rigel

INDUS

TUCANA

Achernar

ERIDANUS

GRUS

PHOENIX

PISCIS
AUSTRINUS

Fomalhaut

CETUS

Mira

AQUARIUS

Orion

Above Orion, the Hunter, was the son of the sea god Poseidon. In one story he fell in love with seven sisters, the Pleiades, and ran after them. In the sky Orion still pursues them – the Pleiades star cluster. Some writers say Orion met his death when he was stung by a scorpion after boasting he could kill any creature on Earth.

Below Canis Major, the Great Dog, contains Sirius, the brightest star in the night sky. Some Greek writers considered it to be the guard dog of the mighty hunter Orion which chased the hare (constellation Lepus) across the heavens. Others thought it was a swift hunting dog named Laelaps.

Canis Major

Right Ophiuchus, the Serpent-Bearer, holds a giant snake in his hands. He represents the Greek god of medicine, Asclepius. The son of Apollo, he was raised and taught by the centaur Chiron. He became a skilled healer. The snake featured in a tale in which he raised someone from the dead; it became a symbol for healing.

Hydra

Ophiuchus

SOUTHERN CONSTELLATIONS: WINTER

Looking North

In the Southern Hemisphere, of course, the seasons are opposite to those in the Northern Hemisphere. So in July it is winter, and in January it is summer. Observers in this hemisphere notice the most changes in the night sky during the year when they look towards the north.

This map of the northern winter sky is quite bare of bright stars. Most prominent are the three stars that in the Northern Hemisphere form the Summer Triangle. They are Vega in Lyra (Lyre), almost due north, Deneb in Cygnus (Swan) and Altair in Aquila (Eagle). This view of Cygnus shows well the shape of a flying swan. Both Cygnus and Aquila lie in the dense starscapes of the Milky Way.

The other star that stands out is Arcturus in Boötes (Herdsman), visible in the west. It is the fourth brightest star in the whole heavens, and has a noticeable orange colour. A familiar northern constellation, Draco (Dragon), can be seen low in the sky. Pegasus (Flying Horse) is just visible over the eastern horizon.

Left A group of galaxies in Virgo. It is part of a huge cluster of galaxies in Virgo and the neighbouring constellation Coma Berenices. Altogether, the cluster contains at least 3,000 galaxies. It is one of the nearest clusters of galaxies.

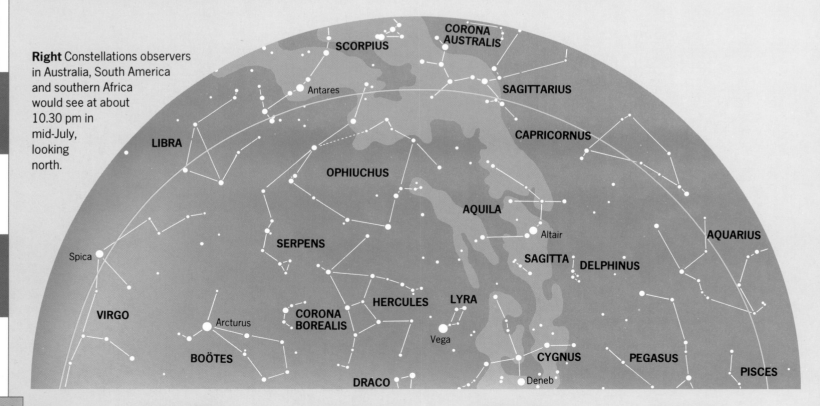

Right Constellations observers in Australia, South America and southern Africa would see at about 10.30 pm in mid-July, looking north.

Above A region of the Milky Way in Norma. It was photographed from New Zealand in 1986 and shows, just below centre, Halley's Comet. The Comet was best seen that year in the Southern Hemisphere. This part of the Milky Way is rich in dense star fields and nebulae.

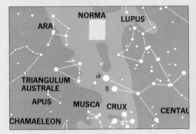

Looking South

The southern aspect of the winter sky makes a startling contrast with the northern. The sky blazes with light from a string of bright stars, most of them set in a brilliant Milky Way. The two brightest are Alpha α and Beta ß Centauri in one of the most magnificent constellations, Centaurus (Centaur).

Alpha Centauri is the closest bright star, being only about 4.3 light-years away. It is only slightly more distant than a neighbouring star, the very faint Proxima Centauri, which is the nearest star to us.

Just below Alpha and Beta Centauri are the four stars of the best-known southern constellation, Crux (Southern Cross). Close to its two brightest stars there appears to be a hole in the Milky Way. It is not a hole, but a dark nebula, a mass of gas and dust that blots out the light from the stars behind. It is known as the Coal Sack. Higher up along the Milky Way, Scorpius can be seen.

In the east, away from the Milky Way, the two brightest stars are Fomalhaut in Piscis Austrinus (Southern Fish) and, closer to the horizon, Achernar. Achernar is the brightest star in Eridanus, a rambling constellation representing a winding river, which extends to Orion, on the celestial equator.

Right Constellations observers in Australia, South America and southern Africa would see at about 10.30 pm in mid-July, looking south.

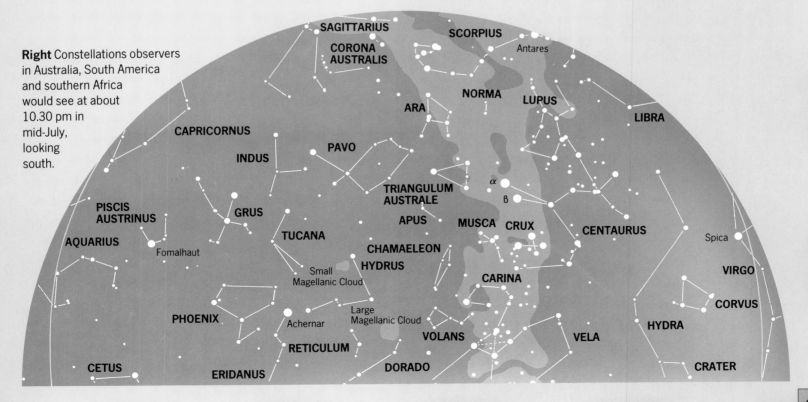

SOUTHERN CONSTELLATIONS: SUMMER

Looking North

This view of the northern sky is much more interesting than the one for July (see page 64). High overhead, just west of the Milky Way, is the brightest star in the heavens. It is Sirius, the Dog Star, in Canis Major (Great Dog).

Lower down and to the west is the bright Rigel, the left foot of the figure of Orion, which appears upside-down in this hemisphere. The bright star that marks Orion's right shoulder is Betelgeuse. Between them are the three stars of Orion's belt. And above the belt is the glowing Orion Nebula.

Lower down is the reddish Aldebaran in Taurus (Bull). It marks the right eye of the bull. Lower still is the prominent naked-eye star cluster, the Pleiades, or Seven Sisters.

On the other side of the Milky Way is the bright Capella. Higher up is the pair of stars Castor and Pollux, in Gemini (Twins). And above them is Procyon, the only bright star in Canis Minor (Little Dog). In the far east Leo (Lion) can be seen. The bright Regulus marks the beast's chest, and the arc of stars its curved neck.

Left The Horsehead Nebula in Orion. It is one of the best known of all the dark nebulae. The easy-to-recognize silhouette of the horse's head is caused by a dense cloud of dust. This blocks the light from the bright nebula behind.

Right Constellations observers in Australia, South America and southern Africa would see at about 10.30 pm in mid-January, looking north.

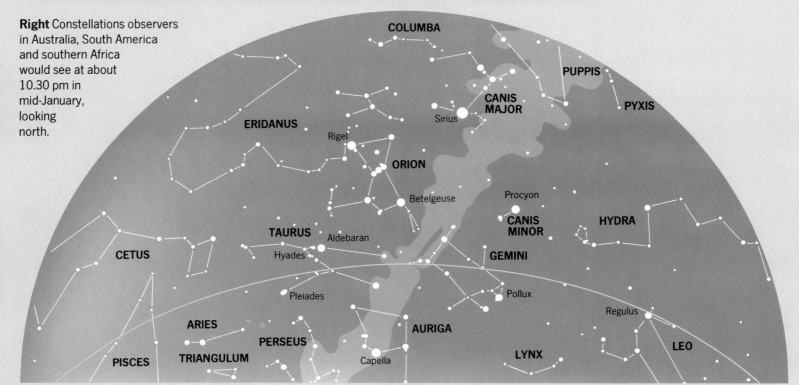

Looking South

This view shows another dazzling display of stars, which explains why stargazing in the Southern Hemisphere is such a pleasure.

Just above the horizon in the south-east is the brilliant pair of stars Alpha α and Beta ß Centauri in Centaurus (Centaur). An arc of less bright stars curves upwards around the cross-shaped Crux (Southern Cross). One of the bright 'stars' in Centaurus is called Omega Centauri. However, it is not a single star but a globular cluster, made up of hundreds of thousands of stars.

Further bright stars dot the Milky Way as it soars upwards, through the constellations Carina (Keel) and Vela (Sails). The brightest star in Carina, seen here due south, is Canopus, which is the second-brightest star in the whole night sky.

A little way below Canopus is a fuzzy patch of light. It looks rather like an isolated bit of the Milky Way or a nebula. But it is neither. A powerful telescope shows it to be another star system, or galaxy. It is called the Large Magellanic Cloud. There is a smaller patch lower down, called the Small Magellanic Cloud. These Clouds which are also called Nubecula Major and Minor, are the nearest galaxies to our own.

Above A peculiar galaxy in Centaurus (Centaur). A dark dust lane appears to cut it in two. Radio astronomers find that this galaxy also gives off powerful radio waves. It is known as Centaurus A.

Right Constellations observers in Australia, South America and southern Africa would see at about 10.30 pm in mid-January, looking south.

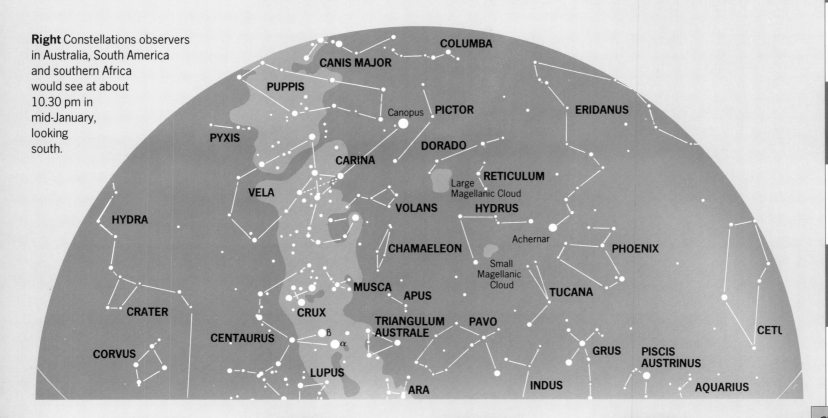

SECTION 4: STARS AND GALAXIES

Stars of every size, colour and brightness shine in the night sky: yellow dwarfs, red giants and blue-white supergiants. One hundred thousand million of them make up our home galaxy, which is rushing, like the other galaxies, headlong through space.

UNDERSTANDING THE STARS

If we could travel through space to the stars, we would find that they are just like our Sun. They are great globes of very hot gas, which give out light, heat and other kinds of radiation. Their energy is produced by nuclear reactions (see page 12).

The Sun is quite a small star, which gives off a yellowish light. We call it a yellow dwarf. There are many stars in the sky like the Sun. There are also many stars that are smaller and many that are bigger; many that are dimmer and many that are brighter.

The biggest stars, called supergiants, are hundreds of times greater in diameter than the Sun. The smallest stars we can see are white dwarfs: some are smaller than the Moon.

Stars may be yellow like the Sun or blue-white, orange or red. Blue-white stars are the hottest, with a surface temperature of over 30,000°C — more than five times as hot as the Sun. Red stars are much cooler than the Sun.

The stars lie far, far away from us — so far that their light takes years to reach us. Even the light from the nearest star, Proxima Centauri, takes over four and a quarter years to reach us. Astronomers say it lies over four and a quarter light-years away. Other stars lie thousands of light-years away.

Right Hundreds of stars and great clouds of glowing gas shown up in this fine picture taken in southern skies. It shows part of the constellation Carina (Keel). The gas clouds surround the star Eta Carinae. Astronomers think this might be the most luminous star in the heavens. It might be as much as 6,000,000 times brighter than our own star, the Sun.

The 'Winking Demon'

The star Algol, in Perseus, is called the Winking Demon. This is because it suddenly dims every 69 hours, as though it has winked.

There are several stars like Algol, called eclipsing binaries. They are binaries, or double stars, made up of two stars circling each other. Algol was the first one to be discovered.

The binary is brightest when both stars are visible (top). It dims when the dark one eclipses, or moves in front of, the bright one (middle). It dims slightly when the bright one eclipses the dim one (bottom).

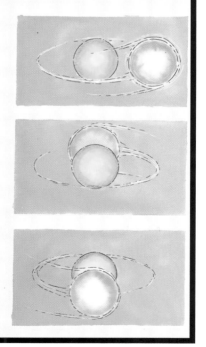

The moving Plough

The stars don't appear to move at all: they seem to be fixed in the heavens. But in fact they are all moving very fast. Aldebaran, for example, is moving away from us at over 800,000 km/h.

We can't see it move because it is too far away.

The bright stars in the Plough are all moving in different directions (right). In 100,000 years time it will look quite different.

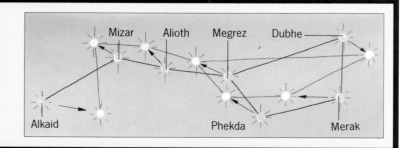

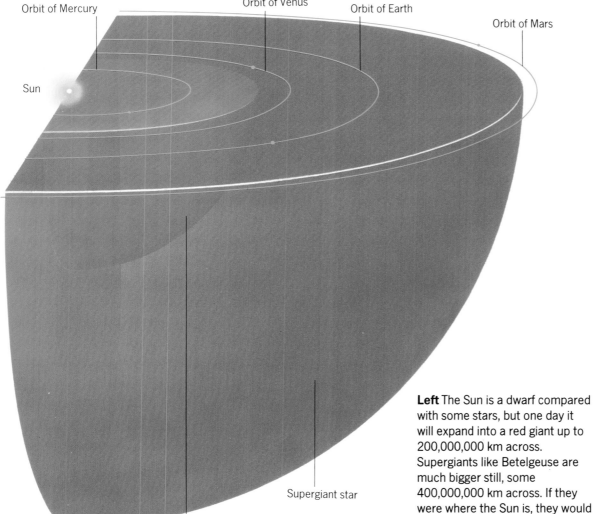

Orbit of Mercury

Orbit of Venus

Orbit of Earth

Orbit of Mars

Sun

Supergiant star

Giant star

Left The Sun is a dwarf compared with some stars, but one day it will expand into a red giant up to 200,000,000 km across. Supergiants like Betelgeuse are much bigger still, some 400,000,000 km across. If they were where the Sun is, they would swallow much of the Solar System.

How bright?

We measure the brightness of stars on a scale of magnitude. On this scale the brightest stars we can see with the naked eye are of the first magnitude (mag 1), and the faintest are of the sixth magnitude (mag 6).

Very bright stars are given a magnitude of less than 1. The brightest star of all, Sirius, has a magnitude of -1.45. Next come Canopus (-0.7) and Alpha Centauri (-0.2).

Faint stars we can see only in binoculars or a telescope are given higher magnitudes than 6. The closest star to us, Proxima Centauri, has a magnitude of 11.

The magnitudes given are a measure of the brightness of the stars as they appear to us. They are apparent magnitudes.

The true brightness of the stars will usually be quite different. This is called their absolute magnitude.

THE STARS: LIFE AND DEATH

To us the stars never seem to change. But they do, over a very long period of time. All the stars we can see will one day die and fade away. But that will not happen yet, because stars live for thousands of millions of years.

Stars begin their life in the clouds of gas and dust we call nebulae (see page 72). A mass of gas and dust suddenly begins to come together under the force of gravity and shrinks in size. As it shrinks, it becomes hotter and hotter until its nuclear furnace lights up (see page 12). Then it starts to shine as a star.

What happens then depends mainly on how big the star is. A star the size of the Sun will shine steadily for about 10,000 million years. Then it will get bigger and bigger until it becomes a red giant star. Later it will shrink until it becomes a white dwarf, not much bigger than a planet.

Stars much bigger than the Sun have a much shorter life and they go out literally with a bang! They shine steadily for a much shorter time and then swell up hundreds of times to become a supergiant star. This soon blasts itself apart in a gigantic explosion we call a supernova. What is left of the star collapses into a tiny, very dense neutron star. Or it carries on collapsing to become a black hole (see pages 82-3).

(see page 72)

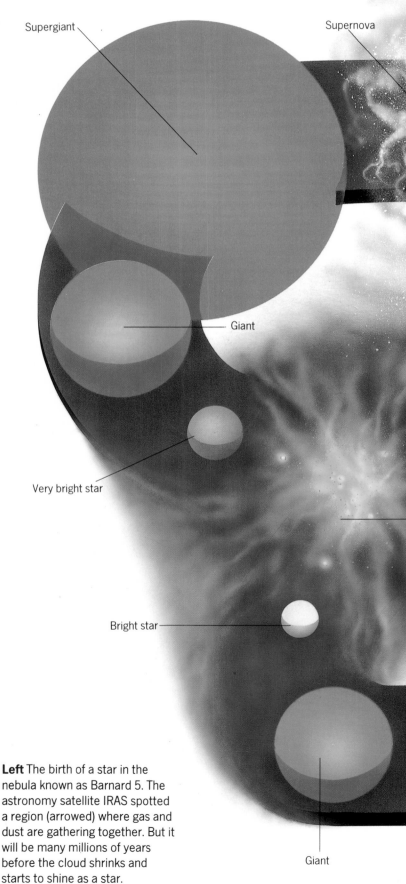

Below Stars of different masses live different lives. They are all born in gas clouds, or nebulae. A star like the Sun (middle) ends up as a white dwarf, a bigger star (bottom) as a pulsar, and a bigger star still (top) as a black hole.

Supergiant

Supernova

Giant

Very bright star

Bright star

Giant

Left The birth of a star in the nebula known as Barnard 5. The astronomy satellite IRAS spotted a region (arrowed) where gas and dust are gathering together. But it will be many millions of years before the cloud shrinks and starts to shine as a star.

Early in the morning of February 24, 1987, astronomer Ian Shelton became the first person for centuries to see a supernova with the naked eye. He was working at the Las Campanas Observatory in Chile. The supernova, SN1987A, took place in the Large Magellanic Cloud, the nearest galaxy to our own. The picture right shows the star (Sanduleak −69° 202) before it exploded. The picture far right shows supernova 1987A at maximum brightness.

HEAVYWEIGHT STAR

Black hole

Left A heavyweight star may have perhaps 10 times more mass than the Sun. It shines brilliantly for a few million years before expanding into a supergiant. This explodes as a supernova and collapses. The force of collapse is so great that all its matter 'disappears'. All that is left is a black hole: a region of enormous gravity.

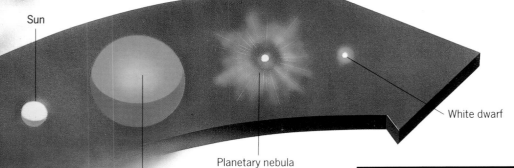

Sun

Giant

Planetary nebula

White dwarf

AVERAGE STAR

Nebula

Left A star like the Sun begins to shine steadily about 50 million years after it has been born in a nebula. It shines steadily for about 10,000 million years before swelling up into a red giant, some 20–30 times bigger. Then it slowly shrinks, puffing off rings of gas as it does so. Finally, it becomes a very dense white dwarf.

Right The Ring Nebula, a beautiful 'smoke ring' of glowing gas in Lyra (Lyre). The ring is made up of gas puffed off by its central, dying star. It is an example of a planetary nebula. This is so called because it looks rather like a planet through a telescope.

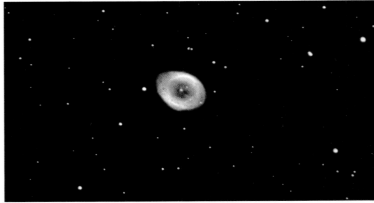

MIDDLEWEIGHT STAR

Left A middleweight star has a mass several times that of the Sun, and it has a much shorter life. It can turn into a red giant in under 100 million years. It expands further into a supergiant, up to 400 million km across. The supergiant explodes, scattering material into space. What is left collapses to form a tiny, neutron star.

Pulsar/neutron star

Supergiant

Supernova

THE STARS: CLUSTERS AND CLOUDS

The Sun travels through space alone. But many stars travel through space with one or more companions. Sometimes tens or hundreds of stars travel through space in a loose group. We call this an open cluster.

The best-known open cluster can easily be seen with the naked eye in the constellation Taurus. It is called the Pleiades, or Seven Sisters. If you have very good eyesight, you should be able to see its six or seven brightest stars. But it contains as many as 200 stars in all.

In some parts of the heavens stars cluster more closely together in their hundreds of thousands. They form a round mass called a globular cluster. In the southern heavens you can see one in the constellation Centaurus with the naked eye, even though it is 160 thousand million million kilometres (16,000 light-years) away.

As well as clusters, colourful 'clouds' can be seen among the constellations. They are great masses of gas and dust, which astronomers call nebulae (one is called a nebula). Some shine because they reflect the light from nearby stars. Others shine because the gas itself gives off light. Sometimes a nebula is not lit up, but blots out the light from stars behind it. Then we call it a dark nebula.

Above The Great Nebula in Orion (Hunter), which is visible to the naked eye. You can see it as a misty patch beneath the three stars that make up Orion's belt. In a telescope it looks magnificent. It is classed as an emission nebula, because its gas emits (gives out) the light that we see.

Below The wispy Veil Nebula in Cygnus (Swan), also called the Cirrus Nebula. It is part of a ring of gas that was given off when a star exploded as a supernova some 50,000 years ago.

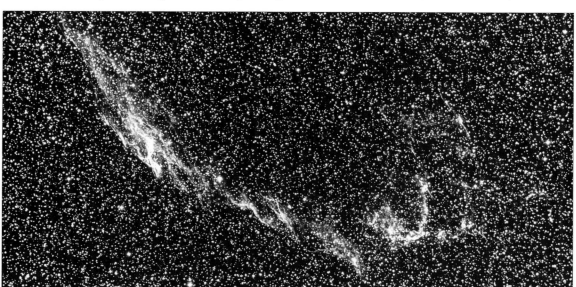

Clouds and stars

In between the stars of the galaxies, there are traces of gas and dust. We call this interstellar matter. The gas is mostly hydrogen, and the dust consists of grains of carbon and rocky material.

In places the matter gets thicker and forms a cloud, or nebula. We can see nebulae in many parts of the heavens. We see nebulae as dark 'holes', where they lie between us and background stars. Some small dark nebulae, called globules, are thicker than usual. One day they might turn into stars.

We see other nebulae when they lie behind a group of stars and reflect their light. These are called reflection nebulae.

Messier objects

In the last century, the French astronomer Charles Messier often mistook star clusters and nebulae for comets, which annoyed him. So he drew up a list of these objects and noted where they were in the heavens.

Astronomers often still use Messier's numbers. For example, the Orion Nebula is also called M42 (number 42 in Messier's list). M1 is the Crab Nebula, the remains of a supernova seen in AD 1054.

M3 is the globular cluster shown above. It is a globe-shaped mass of some 40,000 stars in Canes Venatici (Hunting Dogs).

Below The Jewel Box in Crux (Southern Cross). This fine open cluster of sparkling stars was given its name by John Herschel. He was the son of William, who discovered Uranus. The brightest stars are tens of thousands times brighter than our own Sun.

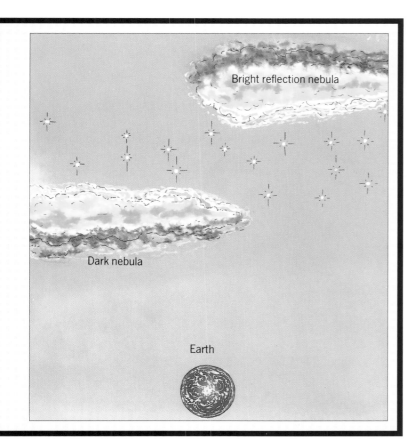

GALAXIES OF STARS

When we look at the night sky, we see it is studded with stars in all directions. It seems as if space is full of stars. In fact it isn't. Stars gather together in space in great star islands, which we call galaxies. There are no stars in the space between the galaxies.

All the stars we see in the sky belong to our Galaxy, which we call the Milky Way. This is the name we also give to the band of light we can see on clear nights arching across the sky. If you look at the Milky Way through a telescope, you can see it is made up of millions upon millions of stars. What you are looking at is a cross-section, or slice, through our Galaxy.

Our Galaxy is shaped like a disc with a bulge in the middle, rather like two fried eggs placed back to back. The stars in the disc lie on arms that curve out from the central bulge. The whole Galaxy rotates, and from a distance would look rather like a flaming Catherine wheel firework.

There are many other galaxies like our own, known as spirals. Other galaxies are round or oval in shape, and are called ellipticals. Irregular galaxies have no particular shape. The nearest galaxies to our own, called the Magellanic Clouds, are irregulars.

Our Galaxy

Seen from the top and the side, these are two very different views of our Galaxy. Containing about 100,000 million stars, it is shaped like a spiral with well-formed arms.

100,000 light-years

Position of Sun

Above The Great Spiral in Andromeda, or the Andromeda Galaxy, M31. This is one of the few galaxies we can see with the naked eye, even though it lies over 2,000,000 light-years away. The Great Spiral is much like our own galaxy, but bigger. Notice it has two small companion galaxies.

Below A map of the whole night sky, made using information sent back by the astronomy satellite IRAS. The white region across the middle is the Milky Way. It is a slice through the disc of our Galaxy. The two white blobs underneath are the two nearest galaxies, the Magellanic Clouds.

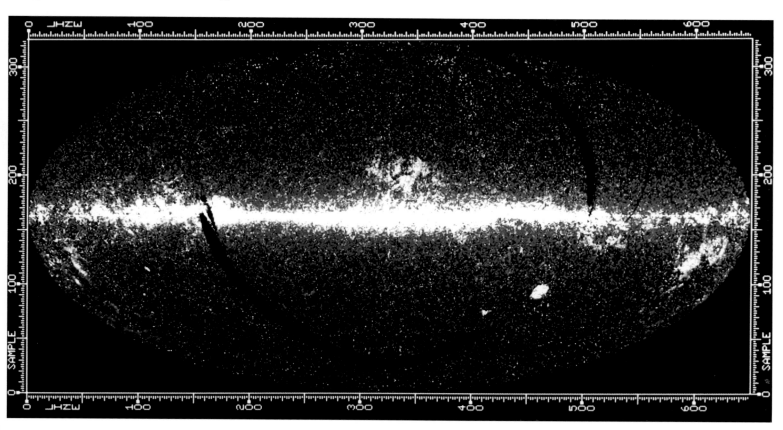

Right There are three main types of regular galaxies: ellipticals, spirals and barred-spirals. The ellipticals vary in shape from round balls to flattened ovals.

Spirals have a bulging centre, with arms curving outwards. They are classed a, b and c, according to how open their arms are. Barred spirals have a bar running through the centre. They are also classed a, b and c.

The astronomer who pioneered study of the galaxies worked out this way of classifying galaxies. He was Edwin Hubble, who worked at Mt Wilson Observatory, in California, USA, in the 1920s.

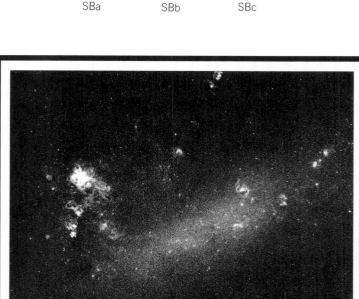

ELLIPTICAL GALAXIES (E)

E0   E3   E5   E7

SPIRAL GALAXIES (S)

Sa   Sb   Sc

BARRED-SPIRAL GALAXIES (SB)

SBa   SBb   SBc

Below Our Galaxy is part of a group, or cluster, of galaxies that occupies our corner of the Universe. The cluster is called the Local Group. It includes our nearest neighbours, the Magellanic Clouds, and the Andromeda Galaxy. In all there are about 30 galaxies in the Local Group. The diagram gives an idea of the way the main galaxies in the Group are gathered together in space.

View from above

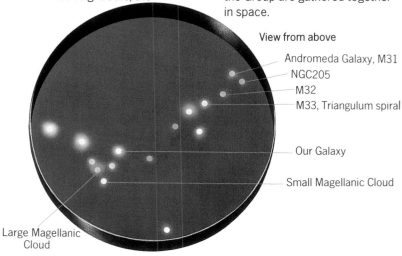

Andromeda Galaxy, M31
NGC205
M32
M33, Triangulum spiral

Our Galaxy

Small Magellanic Cloud

Large Magellanic Cloud

View from the side

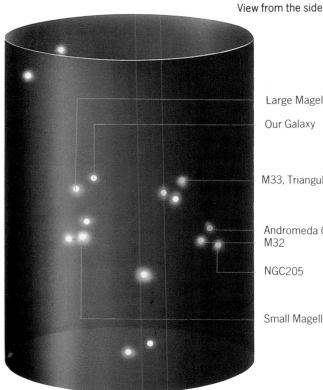

Large Magellanic Cloud

Our Galaxy

M33, Triangulum spiral

Andromeda Galaxy, M31
M32

NGC205

Small Magellanic Cloud

Neighbours

In far southern skies you can see two fuzzy patches, well away from the Milky Way. But like the Milky Way, they are made up of dense masses of stars. They are in fact nearby galaxies. They are known as the Large and Small Magellanic Clouds (LMC and SMC). The LMC is in Dorado (Swordfish); the SMC is in Tucana (Toucan).

The LMC is the closer of the two galaxies, being about 17,000 light-years away. It is a small galaxy, measuring only about 30,000 light-years across .

Above The LMC. The large bright patch on the left is a huge mass of glowing gas called the Tarantula Nebula.

Below Astronauts took this picture of the LMC from the surface of the Moon. It was taken in ultraviolet light.

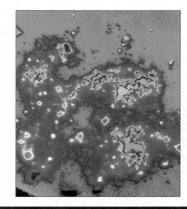

THE EXPANDING UNIVERSE

When astronomers study the outer galaxies, they find that they are all rushing away from us. It seems as if the whole Universe is getting bigger. And astronomers believe that it is. They call this idea the expanding Universe.

They think that the Universe began about 15,000 million years ago in a gigantic explosion called the Big Bang. The newborn Universe was fantastically hot and full of energy. As it expanded, it cooled down and in time hydrogen atoms formed. Very much later the hydrogen gathered into dense clouds, and stars and galaxies began to form. The Universe continued to expand until it became what it is today, the great emptiness of space containing billions of hurtling galaxies.

Astronomers are not sure what will happen to the Universe in the far-distant future. Some believe it will keep on expanding forever until all the stars die and fade away. Others think that one day the Universe will stop expanding, and then begin to shrink. It will get smaller and smaller, until eventually all the stars and galaxies will be squashed together in a 'Big Crunch'. Next, perhaps, could come another Big Bang, which could in turn create a new, expanding Universe. Who knows?

Blowing up the Universe

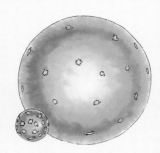

All the outer galaxies are hurtling away from us and from each other in all directions as the Universe expands. You can get an idea of how this expansion works in this simple experiment.

Partly blow up a balloon, and stick some small paper spots on it. Think of them as galaxies, and the surface of the balloon as the Universe. Now blow up the balloon some more. Notice how the galaxies (spots) move away from each other as the Universe (balloon) expands.

Right Most astronomers reckon that the Universe was formed in the Big Bang about 15,000 million years ago, and has been expanding ever since. In the Big Bang all matter, energy and space were created. Nothing existed before the Big Bang, because there was no 'before'. Time itself was created in the Big Bang.

Immediately after the Big Bang (1), the Universe was full of radiation (2). As it expanded and cooled, atomic particles and then atoms formed (3). Eventually, the atoms came together to form the galaxies (4). And the galaxies developed into the state we find them today (5). They will continue to fly apart in the forseeable future (6).

But what will happen in the far-distant future? The Universe may continue to expand forever, getting bigger and bigger (7A, 8A), the galaxies gradually breaking up until nothing is left. This idea is called the Open Universe.

Or the Universe may in time stop expanding, and start getting smaller (7, 8, 9, 10). Eventually, all matter and energy may come together in a Big Crunch, the opposite of the Big Bang. This idea is called the Closed Universe.

8A

The three degrees

Since the Big Bang, the Universe has been cooling down. By now the Universe as a whole should be at a temperature of about 3 degrees above absolute zero (the lowest temperature that can be reached). In 1965 two scientists 'took the temperature' of the Universe. They found it was exactly 3 degrees.

Above Showers of atomic particles. Similar particles were formed seconds after the Big Bang.

Right Two US scientists, Arno Penzias and Robert Wilson 'took the Universe's temperature' using this antenna, in New Jersey.

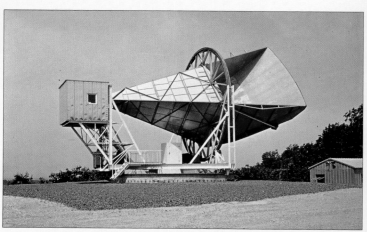

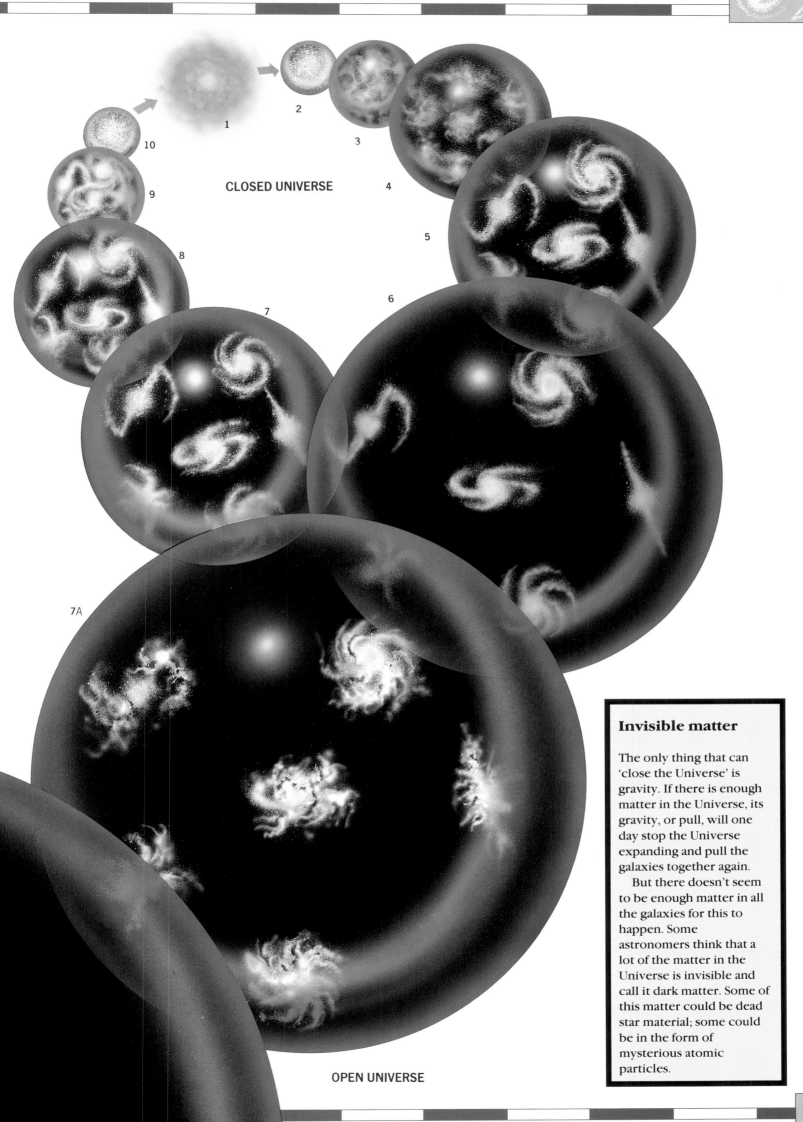

10

1

2

9

3

CLOSED UNIVERSE

4

8

5

7

6

7A

OPEN UNIVERSE

Invisible matter

The only thing that can 'close the Universe' is gravity. If there is enough matter in the Universe, its gravity, or pull, will one day stop the Universe expanding and pull the galaxies together again.

But there doesn't seem to be enough matter in all the galaxies for this to happen. Some astronomers think that a lot of the matter in the Universe is invisible and call it dark matter. Some of this matter could be dead star material; some could be in the form of mysterious atomic particles.

SECTION 5: EXPLORING SPACE

From the ground, astronomers explore the Universe with optical and radio telescopes. From space, they explore it with Earth-orbiting satellites and space probes. Manned spacecraft have already explored our neighbour, the Moon, and seem set to journey to Mars next century.

TELESCOPES

We can learn much about the Moon, stars, planets and comets simply by looking at them just with our eyes. But we can learn much more when we look at them through a telescope.

Telescopes are much better at gathering light than our eyes. They produce bigger, brighter and clearer images than our eyes can. Astronomers use two main types of telescopes. Both produce images that are upside-down. But for viewing the heavenly bodies, this doesn't really matter.

One type of telescope uses mirrors to gather the light and focus it into a sharp image. It is called a reflector because mirrors reflect light. All the biggest telescopes are reflectors. One in Russia had a mirror 6 metres across. It is so sensitive that it could detect the light from a candle 25,000 kilometres away!

The other type of telescope uses glass lenses to gather and focus light. It is called a refractor because lenses refract, or bend light. Many people begin studying the heavens with binoculars, which are much cheaper than telescopes. A pair of binoculars is a kind of double refractor, with a separate telescope for each eye. Unlike a telescope, it produces images that are the right way up.

Above The first of the giant telescopes, the famous Hooker 100-inch (2.5-m) telescope at Mt Wilson Observatory in California. It was completed in 1917, and was used by Edwin Hubble and Milton Humason in their pioneering studies of the galaxies.

A megalithic marvel

Four thousand years ago the Ancient Britons were using a circle of massive stones, or megaliths, as an astronomical 'instrument'. We know it today as Stonehenge, on Salisbury Plain. The stones were laid out to mark the positions of the Sun and Moon.

The picture shows part of the outer ring of 'sarsen' stones lined up with the distant 'heel' stone. The point where the heel stone touches the horizon marks where the Sun rises on June 21 each year. This is midsummer's day, or the summer solstice.

The pioneers

A Dutch lens-maker, Hans Lippershey, invented the lens-type, refracting telescope in 1608. A year later the Italian Galileo built a refractor. He was the first to train one on the heavens. He observed Venus and Jupiter's moons.

The early refractors suffered from blurred images. To avoid this, the English scientist Isaac Newton built a mirror-type, reflecting telescope in about 1668.

Refractors and reflectors

A refractor uses two sets of lenses to gather and focus the light from an object. The objective lens forms an image of the object, which is then viewed through the eyepiece.

Reflectors use a curved mirror to gather the light. Other mirrors reflect it to a point where an eyepiece, at the side or underneath, can view the image.

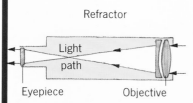

Refractor

Light path

Eyepiece   Objective

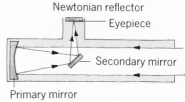

Newtonian reflector

Eyepiece

Secondary mirror

Primary mirror

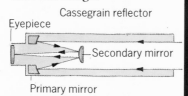

Cassegrain reflector

Eyepiece

Secondary mirror

Primary mirror

Above A fine modern telescope, the Kapteyn 1-m reflector at the Roque de los Muchachos Observatory on La Palma, in the Canary Islands. It is a relatively lightweight instrument, which makes widespread use of electronics and is designed for computer control.

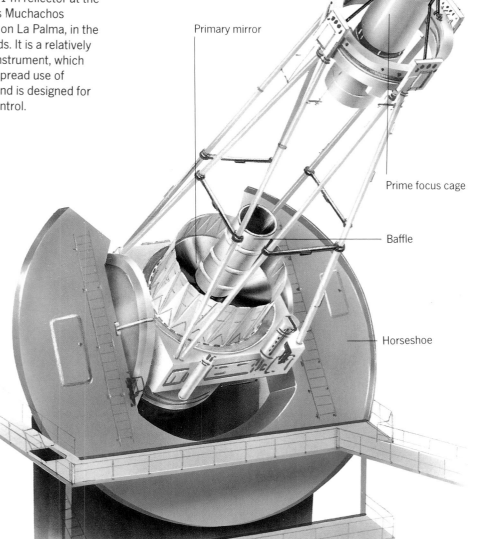

Primary mirror

Prime focus cage

Baffle

Horseshoe

Left The Anglo-Australian Telescope, at Siding Spring Observatory in New South Wales, Australia. It is a reflector with a 3.9-m diameter mirror. The open body tube is mounted inside a huge and well-named horseshoe bearing. This rotates the telescope to follow the stars. The prime-focus cage is located nearly 13 m above the mirror. It is big enough for an astronomer to ride in! Observations may be made from the cage or, via mirrors, from a number of other positions.

Below An amateur astronomer explains how his 21-cm telescope works. It is a Newtonian reflector, which has a viewing eyepiece near the top of the body tube. It has a small brass 'finder-scope' to help him direct the telescope to the right part of the heavens.

Binoculars

Observing the night sky through a pair of binoculars is a delight. Glittering starry vistas open up that you can't appreciate with the naked eye.

Each binocular tube is a compact refractor, with an objective and an eyepiece. In between, the light path is 'folded' by the use of a pair of reflecting prisms.

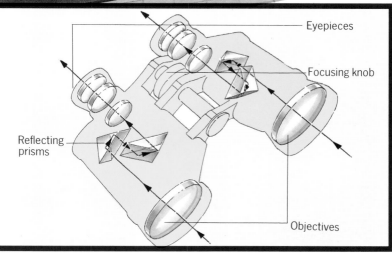

Eyepieces

Focusing knob

Reflecting prisms

Objectives

ASTRONOMICAL OBSERVATIONS

Astronomers work in observatories. That is where they observe the heavens through their telescopes. Amateur astronomers may use a shed in their back garden as an observatory. But professional astronomers use big dome-shaped buildings to house their telescopes.

Most big observatories are located high up in the mountains far away from city lights. At such heights the air is clearer and more still than it is lower down. At most observatories there are several domes, housing telescopes of different sizes. Some have special solar telescopes to observe the Sun.

At night astronomers open the domes and point the telescopes towards the parts of the sky they wish to observe. They use the telescopes as giant cameras and take pictures of the stars on photographic film. Because the stars are faint, they usually expose the film for several hours, sometimes all night. The telescopes are driven slowly round by motors so that they follow the stars as they circle overhead (see page 78).

At some observatories astronomers gather and study the radio waves coming from the stars and galaxies. They use huge metal dishes as radio telescopes. From the signals they receive, they can produce radio 'pictures'.

Imaging the Sun

By observing the Sun, we are taking a close look at an ordinary star. Everything that happens on the Sun affects us here on Earth.

But the surface of the Sun is so bright that it cannot be looked at with telescopes in the ordinary way. Solar telescopes that project (throw) the image must be used instead. The biggest one is the McMath Solar Telescope at Kitt Peak National Observatory in Arizona, pictured above.

The diagram below shows how it is built. Three mirrors are used in turn to reflect sunlight and project an image on to a table in the observing room.

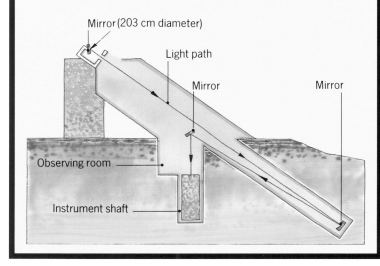

Mirror (203 cm diameter)

Light path

Mirror

Mirror

Observing room

Instrument shaft

Left A collection of telescopes at the Roque de los Muchachos Observatory. This expanding European observatory is located on the island of La Palma, in the Canary Islands. It is built on a mountaintop above the clouds, where it has clear views of the heavens on all but a few nights a year.

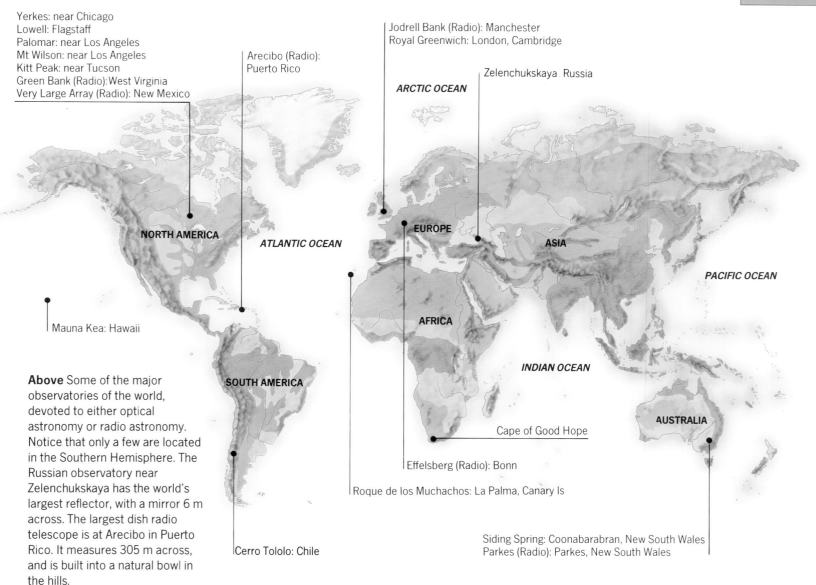

Yerkes: near Chicago
Lowell: Flagstaff
Palomar: near Los Angeles
Mt Wilson: near Los Angeles
Kitt Peak: near Tucson
Green Bank (Radio): West Virginia
Very Large Array (Radio): New Mexico

Arecibo (Radio): Puerto Rico

Jodrell Bank (Radio): Manchester
Royal Greenwich: London, Cambridge

Zelenchukskaya. Russia

ARCTIC OCEAN

NORTH AMERICA

ATLANTIC OCEAN

EUROPE

ASIA

PACIFIC OCEAN

AFRICA

INDIAN OCEAN

Mauna Kea: Hawaii

SOUTH AMERICA

Cape of Good Hope

AUSTRALIA

Effelsberg (Radio): Bonn

Roque de los Muchachos: La Palma, Canary Is

Cerro Tololo: Chile

Siding Spring: Coonabarabran, New South Wales
Parkes (Radio): Parkes, New South Wales

Above Some of the major observatories of the world, devoted to either optical astronomy or radio astronomy. Notice that only a few are located in the Southern Hemisphere. The Russian observatory near Zelenchukskaya has the world's largest reflector, with a mirror 6 m across. The largest dish radio telescope is at Arecibo in Puerto Rico. It measures 305 m across, and is built into a natural bowl in the hills.

Radio astronomy

Stars give out many other kinds of rays besides light. They include gamma rays, X-rays, ultraviolet rays, infrared rays and radio waves.

A US radio engineer named Karl Jansky first detected radio waves coming from the heavens in 1931. Study of these waves is now one of the most exciting branches of astronomy.

Astronomers build large radio telescopes to gather the faint radio waves that come from outer space. Most common is the dish type. The dish picks up the waves and reflects them on to an antenna above. The signals pass to a radio receiver.

Left The radio telescope at Parkes, New South Wales, Australia, has a dish 64 m across. It is often used to study quasars.

Above The radio waves coming from the Whirlpool Galaxy in Canes Venatici (Hunting Dogs) were used to produce this false-colour image.

SPACE SATELLITES

In their telescopes, astronomers cannot view the heavens as clearly as they would like. This is because they are looking through a 'dirty window' – the Earth's atmosphere. The atmosphere is full of dust and moisture, and it shimmers with air currents. All this stops astronomers seeing clearly.

However, they can now overcome this problem by sending telescopes above the atmosphere into space on satellites. The Russians launched the first satellite, Sputnik 1, in 1957. The first successful astronomy satellites were launched a few years later.

Above the atmosphere, astronomy satellites not only see the objects in space more clearly, they also look at them in different ways. They can collect the invisible rays the stars and galaxies give out, such as X-rays, ultraviolet and infrared. Astronomers cannot study these rays from the ground because the atmosphere blocks them.

Astronomy satellites have made many exciting discoveries in recent years and have given astronomers much new information about what the Universe is really like. For example, X-ray satellites like Einstein have spied regions where there could be those awesome bodies called black holes (see page 70). An infrared satellite called IRAS has spotted clouds where stars were being born.

Rockets and orbits

The Earth's gravity is very strong. To beat it, a satellite has to be launched from the Earth at a speed of 28,000 km/h. Only one engine is powerful enough to boost anything to that speed – the rocket. Rockets can work in space because they are self-contained. They carry not only fuel, but also the oxygen to burn the fuel.

Even so, a single rocket engine is not by itself powerful enough to get into space. Several have to be joined together, with each one firing in turn to boost the ones above faster and higher. This arrangement is called a step rocket.

In space, satellites circle round and round the Earth in a path, or orbit, at least 200 km high to avoid the atmosphere. Some travel over the poles (polar orbit), others over the Equator (equatorial orbit). In an equatorial orbit 35,900 km high, a satellite laps the Earth in 24 hours. In this geostationary orbit the satellite appears fixed in the sky.

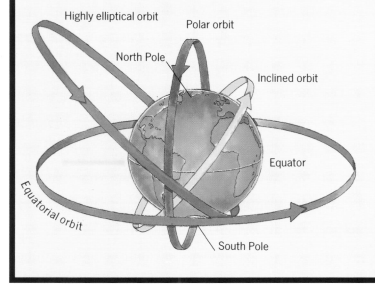

Second stage drops away; third stage fires

First stage drops away; second stage fires

Lift-off

Highly elliptical orbit

Polar orbit

North Pole

Inclined orbit

Equatorial orbit

Equator

South Pole

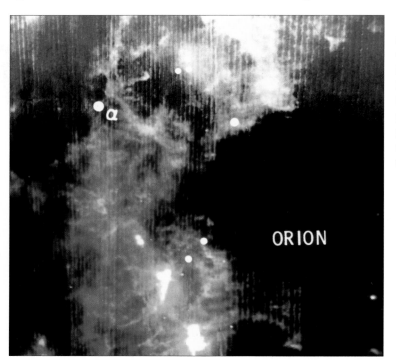

ORION

Left A picture of Orion (Hunter) and part of the neighbouring constellation Monoceros (Unicorn). It was taken by the Infrared Astronomy Satellite, IRAS. The letter α shows the position of the star Betelgeuse. The picture is remarkable because it shows that Orion is embedded in a vast cloud of dust and gas.

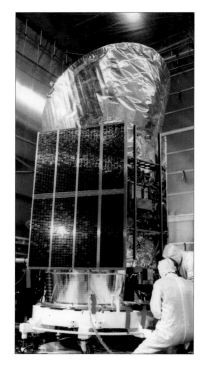

Right US and Dutch engineers carrying out the final checks on IRAS, which was launched in January 1983. For ten months it tuned into the infrared radiation given out by the heavens. It spied regions where stars were being born and found several comets.

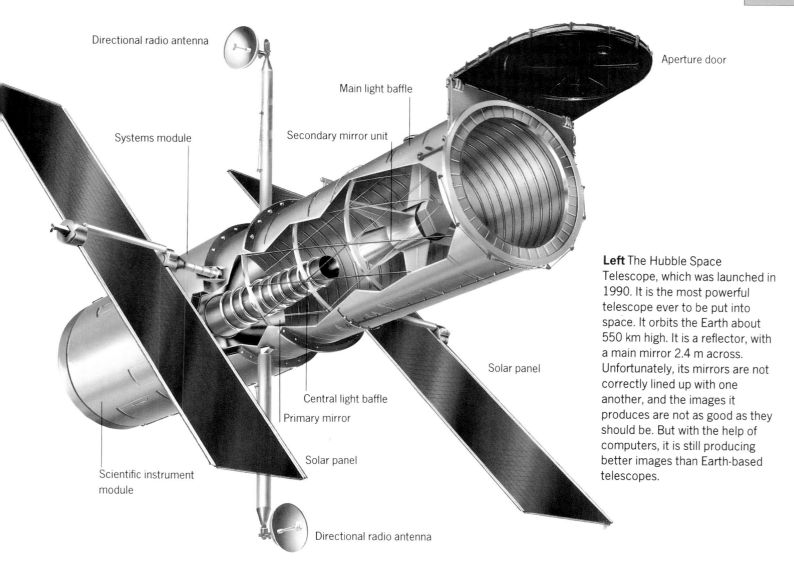

Directional radio antenna

Main light baffle

Systems module

Secondary mirror unit

Aperture door

Solar panel

Central light baffle

Primary mirror

Scientific instrument module

Solar panel

Directional radio antenna

Left The Hubble Space Telescope, which was launched in 1990. It is the most powerful telescope ever to be put into space. It orbits the Earth about 550 km high. It is a reflector, with a main mirror 2.4 m across. Unfortunately, its mirrors are not correctly lined up with one another, and the images it produces are not as good as they should be. But with the help of computers, it is still producing better images than Earth-based telescopes.

Left Mars, as pictured by the Hubble Space Telescope. The colour image was produced from separate images taken through colour filters. North is to the top left. The picture shows a northern ice cap, with blue haze above it.

The prominent dark feature in the middle of the disc is the region Syrtis Major. The bright circular patch underneath is Hellas, a huge basin caused by the impact of a meteorite long, long ago.

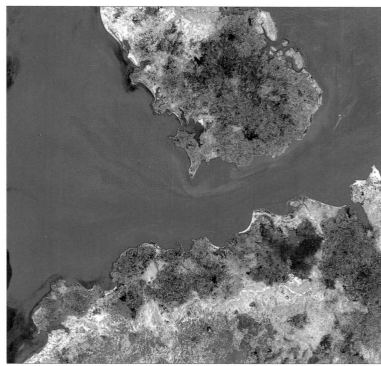

Right An image of part of China, produced from signals sent back by the first successful Earth-survey satellite. This was NASA's first ERTS (Earth Resources Technology Satellite), later called Landsat 1. Five Landsats were launched between 1972 and 1984. They scanned the Earth in light of different colours. The signals they sent back carried all kinds of information about the surface. From this data, scientists could, for example, spot new mineral deposits, diseased crops and water pollution.

SPACE PROBES

Satellites travel in space, but they are still gripped by Earth's powerful gravity. Other spacecraft, however, can break free of gravity completely and journey to the Moon and the distant planets. They are called space probes. To escape, probes have to be launched with a speed of at least 11 kilometres a second, or 40,000 kilometres an hour. This speed is called Earth's escape velocity.

Above A Titan-Centaur rocket blasts off from Cape Canaveral in Florida, carrying the Voyager 1 probe. It is September 1977. In 18 months time it will be looping round Jupiter at a speed of 135,000 km/h.

Right The Voyager probe carries a variety of instruments to investigate the planets and their environment. It has two TV cameras to take pictures, mounted on a movable scan platform. Its dish radio antenna is 3.7 m across.

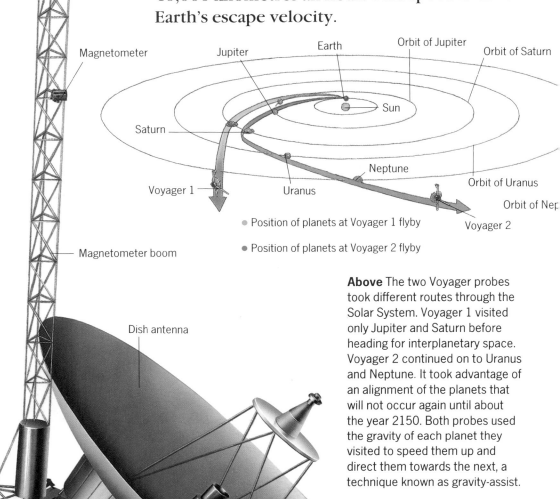

- Position of planets at Voyager 1 flyby
- Position of planets at Voyager 2 flyby

Magnetometer

Jupiter

Earth

Orbit of Jupiter

Orbit of Saturn

Saturn

Sun

Magnetometer boom

Voyager 1

Uranus

Neptune

Orbit of Uranus

Orbit of Nep

Voyager 2

Dish antenna

Nuclear battery

Radio astronomy antenna

Decagon systems unit

Thrusters

Science instrument boom

Cosmic ray detector

Charged particle detector

Infrared instrument

Scan platform

Plasma detector

TV cameras

Above The two Voyager probes took different routes through the Solar System. Voyager 1 visited only Jupiter and Saturn before heading for interplanetary space. Voyager 2 continued on to Uranus and Neptune. It took advantage of an alignment of the planets that will not occur again until about the year 2150. Both probes used the gravity of each planet they visited to speed them up and direct them towards the next, a technique known as gravity-assist.

Left Each Voyager carries a record disc like this, called the Sounds of Earth. It features words, music and images from planet Earth to enlighten any alien beings who may one day come across it.

To begin with, space scientists found it difficult to send probes to the Moon, only about 385,000 kilometres away. That was in 1959. But now they are able to send probes thousands of millions of kilometres to a close encounter with the farthest planets in our Solar System, such as Uranus and Neptune.

Sending a probe to a far-distant planet is very difficult. After escaping from Earth's gravity, it must be aimed very carefully. It must be directed at a point in space in the planet's orbit, so that it will arrive there at the same time as the planet. This could be in several years time. It took 12 years for Voyager 2 to meet Neptune in its orbit.

Communicating with probes is another problem. They travel so far away that their radio signals can take hours to reach Earth. By then the signals are incredibly faint. But by using big dish aerials and computers, scientists can pick up the faint signals and convert them into brilliant pictures.

Above The Russian Moon-walker Lunokhod, which the probe Luna 17 landed on the Moon in 1970. It carried TV cameras and instruments to investigate the lunar surface. Early next century a similar machine may be trundling about on Mars, to prepare for a manned landing later.

Calling long- distance

When Voyager 2 flew past Neptune in 1989, its signals took 4 hours 6 minutes to reach us.

Because of such time-lags probes can't be controlled directly by radio from Earth. They are controlled by the computers they carry. Instructions are fed into the computers before launch and while the probes are cruising towards their target.

The picture shows one of the huge dish aerials NASA uses to communicate with its probes.

Looping the loop

In 1989 the probe Galileo was launched from the space shuttle (left). It is now on its way to Jupiter by a most roundabout route. The plan is as follows. After launch, it heads for Venus. It loops round the planet and back to Earth. In turn it loops round Earth, then heads for the asteroid belt. It loops back to the Earth yet again before finally making for Jupiter.

Galileo should reach the planet in 1995. The main craft will go into orbit, while a probe will be dropped into the thick atmosphere.

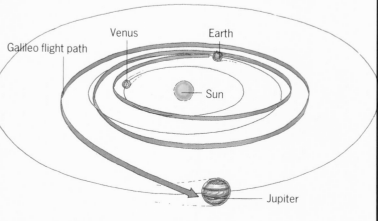

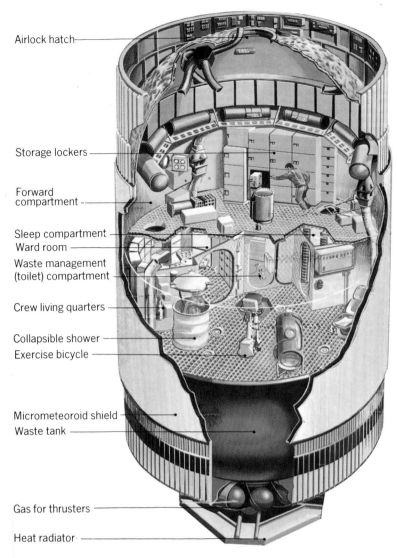

Airlock hatch

Storage lockers

Forward compartment

Sleep compartment
Ward room
Waste management (toilet) compartment

Crew living quarters

Collapsible shower
Exercise bicycle

Micrometeoroid shield
Waste tank

Gas for thrusters

Heat radiator

MANNED SPACE FLIGHT

Human beings first went into space in 1961, less than four years after the Space Age began. The first astronauts flew in cramped 'capsules' as test pilots, exploring the dangerous and unknown space frontier.

In the early days, no one knew whether flesh-and-blood human beings could stand up to travelling in space for long. But it soon became clear that they could. And in 1965 astronauts began 'walking' in space – floating outside their spacecraft in spacesuits. They called this EVA, or extravehicular activity.

By now Russia and the United States had begun a race to land the first person on the Moon. The United States won the race in July 1969, when two Apollo 11 astronauts

Above A view inside the orbital workshop, the largest part of Skylab. The workshop provided the main living and working space for the crew. It was built using a rocket casing left over from the Apollo Moon-landing project.

Right Skylab astronauts snapped the space station as they began their journey back to Earth in February 1974. They had spent a record 84 days in space. Two other teams had earlier spent 28 and 59 days in the space station.

Above A bronze bust of Yuri Gagarin at the Cosmonaut Training Centre in Star City, Moscow.

Space pioneers

April 12, 1961 Russian pilot Yuri Gagarin makes the first manned spaceflight in Vostok 1.
February 20, 1962 John Glenn becomes the first American in orbit, in Friendship 7.
June 16, 1963 Valentina Tereshkova (Russia) becomes the first woman in space in Vostok 6.
March 18, 1965 Alexei Leonov (Russia) makes the first spacewalk from Voshkod 2.
June 3, 1965 Edward White makes the first American spacewalk from Gemini 4.

Above John Glenn enters the capsule of Friendship 7.

Right Valentina Tereshkova.

March 16, 1966 Neil Armstrong and David Scott in Gemini 8 carry out the first docking in space.
December 21, 1968 Frank Borman, James Lovell and William Anders in Apollo 10 set out to travel to the Moon and back. They become the

planted their footsteps in the lunar soil
(see page 88). Apollo was the name of the US
Moon-landing project.

A few years later, Russia and the United
States launched the first space stations. These
craft were designed to stay in space a long time
so that astronauts could carry out useful
scientific work there.

Early in 1974, three astronauts returned to
Earth fit and well after spending three months
in the US space station Skylab. Ten years later
cosmonauts (the Russian word for astronauts)
in Russia's Salyut space stations were staying in
orbit for up to eight months without coming to
any harm. In 1986 Russia launched a new space
station, called Mir (meaning 'Peace'). In this
craft cosmonauts have spent over a year in
space.

Below Russia's space station Mir, as it looked in the early 1990s. The base unit was launched in February 1986. It provides the main living quarters for the crew. The Kvant 1 module (foreground), and the Kvant 2 and Kristall modules, are now linked with it. The main scientific work of the station is carried out in these modules. On the right of the station is a Soyuz spacecraft. This ferries cosmonauts to and from orbit. On the left is a Progress spacecraft. It carries mail, equipment and fresh supplies to the crew in residence.

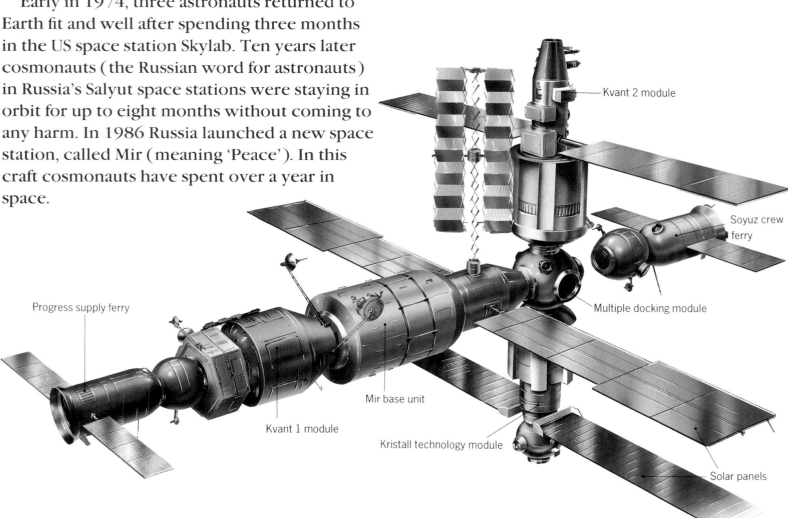

Kvant 2 module

Soyuz crew ferry

Progress supply ferry

Multiple docking module

Mir base unit

Kvant 1 module

Kristall technology module

Solar panels

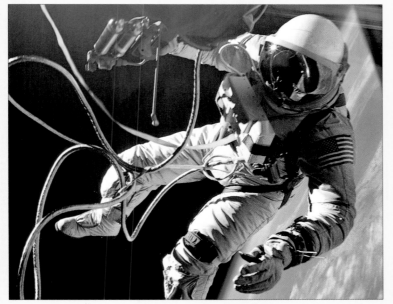

first people to escape from the Earth's gravity.

July 20, 1969 Neil Armstrong and Edwin Aldrin from Apollo 11 walk on the moon for two-and-a-half hours. Michael Collins stays in orbit in the CSM.

May 25, 1973 Charles Conrad, Joseph Kerwin and Paul Weitz make the first visit to Skylab, nearly destroyed during launch.

July 17, 1975 Astronauts and cosmonauts shake hands in orbit during the Apollo-Soyuz Test Project (ASTP).

Left Tumbling head over heels, Edward White makes the first US spacewalk from Gemini 4.

Above Apollo 11 astronaut Edwin Aldrin about to become the second man to walk on the Moon.

EXPLORING THE MOON

July 20, 1969, is one of the most memorable dates in history. On that date a US astronaut in a white spacesuit stepped down from his spacecraft on to the Moon. 'That's one small step for man,' he said, 'one giant leap for mankind.' It was the first time a human being had set foot on another world.

The astronaut was Neil Armstrong, who had travelled to the Moon in the Apollo 11 spacecraft. He was soon joined by Edwin Aldrin, and together they explored the Moon on foot. They picked up samples of rock and soil, set up experiments, and took photographs of the stunning landscape.

Over the next three and a half years, five more landings were made on the Moon, and ten more astronauts trod the lunar soil. They explored different regions of the Moon: flat 'seas', rugged highlands and spectacular valleys. The astronauts on the last three missions were able to travel much farther because they had a vehicle called the lunar rover, or Moon buggy.

Eugene Cernan was the commander of the last Moon-landing mission, Apollo 17. As he left the Moon on December 14, 1972, he promised: 'God willing, we shall return with peace and hope for all mankind'.

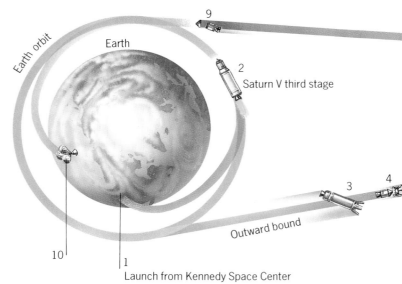

Earth orbit

Earth

9

2 Saturn V third stage

3 4

Outward bound

10

1

Launch from Kennedy Space Center

Apollo lunar module

This part of the Apollo spacecraft was designed to land two astronauts on the Moon. Made in two parts, the lower part was used as a launch pad for the upper one when the astronauts left the Moon. The picture shows the first flight model of the lunar module in Earth orbit during the Apollo 9 mission. It was named Spider.

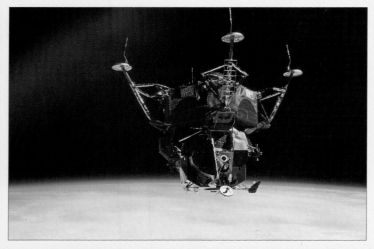

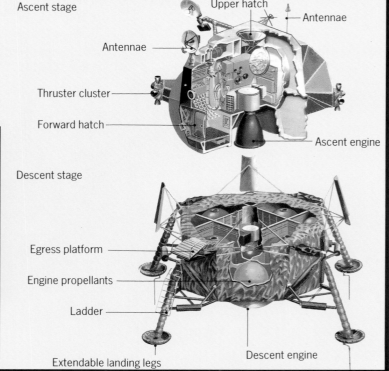

Ascent stage

Upper hatch

Antennae

Antennae

Thruster cluster

Forward hatch

Ascent engine

Descent stage

Egress platform

Engine propellants

Ladder

Extendable landing legs

Descent engine

Left Second man on the Moon Edwin Aldrin and the lunar module Eagle. They stand on the flat and desolate Sea of Tranquillity during the pioneering Apollo 11 mission. As at the other landing sites, the ground is covered with fine dust.

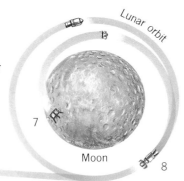

Lunar orbit

Homeward bound

Moon

7

8

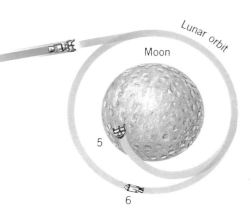

Lunar orbit

Moon

5

6

Above A panorama of photographs covering the spectacular Apollo 15 landing site. The lunar module, Falcon, set down in the foothills of the Apennine mountain range. The astronaut working in the picture is mission commander David Scott.

Left The flight plan for the Apollo missions. The spacecraft was launched (1) by a Saturn V rocket, 111 m high. It entered orbit with the third rocket stage (2). This fired to boost the spacecraft to the Moon, then separated (3). The spacecraft (4), made up of the command and service modules (CSM) and lunar module (LM), went into lunar orbit. The LM landed (5), while the CSM stayed in orbit (6).

The top half of the LM left the Moon (7) and docked with the CSM (8). The CSM's engines fired to send it back to Earth. There, the command (crew) module separated (9), then parachuted down for an ocean landing (10).

Unlucky thirteenth

There were six successful Apollo landings: Apollo 11 (July 1969), 12 (November 1969), 14 (January 1971), 15 (July 1971), 16 (April 1972) and 17 (December 1972).

There should have been a landing by Apollo 13 (April 1970) but it was damaged by an explosion on the way to the Moon. The crew had to use their lunar module as a 'liferaft' to make it safely back to Earth.

Moon buggy

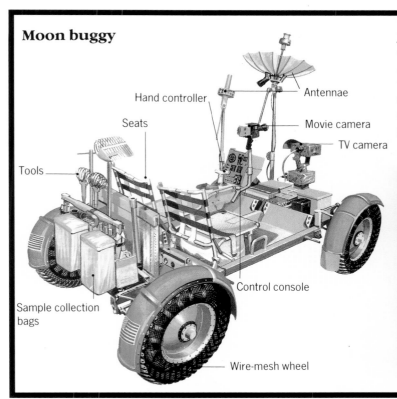

Hand controller

Antennae

Seats

Movie camera

TV camera

Tools

Sample collection bags

Control console

Wire-mesh wheel

John Young kicks up Moon dust as he test drives the Apollo 16 Moon buggy. It was a collapsible vehicle, able to carry two astronauts and their equipment. It was powered by electric motors, one on each wheel. Its top speed was about 15 km/h. The three buggies used, on the Apollo 15, 16 and 17 missions, together covered a distance of more than 90 km.

TOWARDS TOMORROW

In the early days of space flight, launching rockets and spacecraft could be used only once. This was very wasteful and expensive. But in April 1981 a new kind of launching craft rocketed into orbit. It was Columbia, a winged spaceship called a space shuttle. Seven months later Columbia was rocketing into the heavens again. It was the first time any craft had returned to Earth and been relaunched.

Columbia was the first of a fleet of US space-shuttle craft, which can return to space again and again. The other members of the fleet are Discovery, Atlantis and Endeavour. These craft carry a crew of up to seven, male and female, and are used mainly for launching satellites and space probes. They also carry into orbit on occasions a fully equipped space laboratory called Spacelab. It has been designed by the European Space Agency (ESA).

Soon, shuttles will carry into orbit parts for a large space station called Freedom. Astronaut-engineers will then join the parts together. When Freedom goes into operation, shuttle craft will visit it regularly, bringing new crews and fresh supplies.

Early next century astronaut-engineers will start building lunar ferries, spacecraft designed to travel to the Moon and back. The ferries will transport scientists and engineers, who will set up a permanent base on the Moon. Later, interplanetary craft will be built to carry astronauts to explore Mars. One day, perhaps, interstellar craft will be built to carry people to other worlds among the stars.

Above The space shuttle orbiter Challenger in orbit in June 1983. Inside the open payload bay are two pods containing satellites, ready to be launched.

Right The space shuttle orbiter. It takes off like a rocket; acts like a spacecraft in orbit; then returns to Earth like a plane. It is 37 m long, and has a wingspan of nearly 24 m. Three main rocket engines in the tail pod fire at lift-off. They take their fuel from a separate tank. Two smaller engines in the pod are fired in orbit to speed up or brake the orbiter.

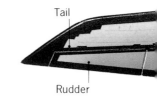

Tail

Rudder

Moon base

Early next century human beings will return to the Moon, and stay. They will explore the Moon more fully, and set up scientific laboratories and astronomical observatories. The far side of the Moon would be a good site for a radio observatory, for example. It would be shielded from interference from Earth.

To begin with, the Moon-dwellers will live in empty rocket cases. Then they will build permanent living quarters, mostly underground. They will mine the Moon for building materials and for minerals which they will process into metals.

Left A processing plant on the Moon next century. It extracts oxygen from rocks.

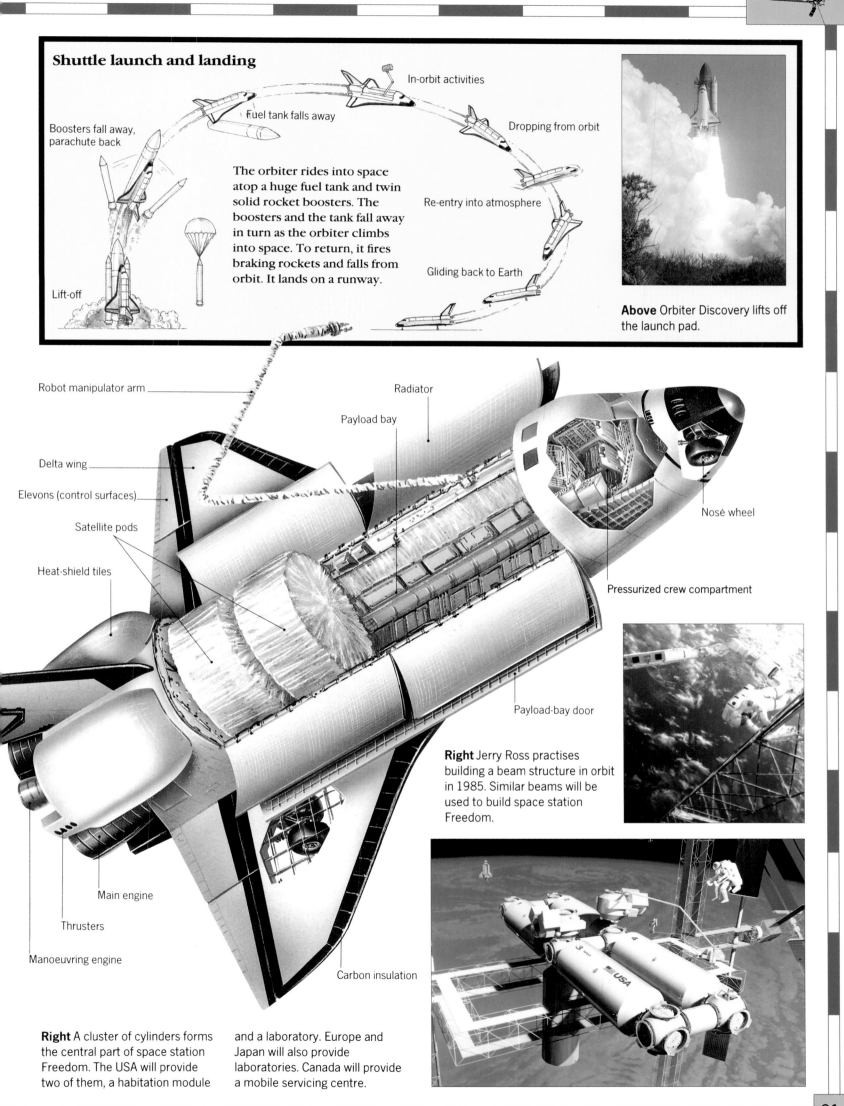

Shuttle launch and landing

In-orbit activities

Fuel tank falls away

Boosters fall away,
parachute back

Dropping from orbit

The orbiter rides into space
atop a huge fuel tank and twin
solid rocket boosters. The
boosters and the tank fall away
in turn as the orbiter climbs
into space. To return, it fires
braking rockets and falls from
orbit. It lands on a runway.

Re-entry into atmosphere

Gliding back to Earth

Lift-off

Above Orbiter Discovery lifts off
the launch pad.

Robot manipulator arm

Radiator

Payload bay

Delta wing

Elevons (control surfaces)

Nose wheel

Satellite pods

Heat-shield tiles

Pressurized crew compartment

Payload-bay door

Right Jerry Ross practises
building a beam structure in orbit
in 1985. Similar beams will be
used to build space station
Freedom.

Main engine

Thrusters

Manoeuvring engine

Carbon insulation

Right A cluster of cylinders forms
the central part of space station
Freedom. The USA will provide
two of them, a habitation module
and a laboratory. Europe and
Japan will also provide
laboratories. Canada will provide
a mobile servicing centre.

GLOSSARY

A

airlock: a chamber in a spacecraft from which the air can be removed. Astronauts pass through an airlock when they go spacewalking.

artificial satellite: an object that circles the Earth in space.

asteroid: a small object made of rock and metal that orbits in the Solar System between Mars and Jupiter.

astrology: a study that tries to link happenings in people's lives with the positions of the stars and planets in the heavens.

astronaut: someone who travels in space. The Russian term for an astronaut is cosmonaut.

astronautics: the study of space travel.

astronomy: the science that studies the stars, the planets and all the other heavenly bodies.

atmosphere: the layer of gases around the Earth or another heavenly body.

atmospheric pressure: the weight of the atmosphere as it presses on the Earth's surface.

atomic particles: particles that are found in the atom, the tiniest bit of matter that can exist. They include the electron, proton and neutron. Protons and neutrons are found in the nucleus, or centre, of the atom. Electrons circle around the nucleus.

aurora: a colourful glow seen in far northern and far southern skies, also known as the Northern and Southern Lights.

B

Big Bang: an event that astronomers believe happened some 15,000 million years ago which created the Universe.

black hole: a region in space that has such enormous gravity that not even light rays can escape.

C

celestial sphere: an imaginary dark globe surrounding the Earth. The stars appear to be fixed to the inside of the globe.

comet: a tiny member of the Solar System, which starts to shine when it draws near to the Sun.

constellation: the pattern a group of bright stars make in the sky.

cosmic rays: atomic particles that bombard the Earth from space.

cosmonaut: the Russian term for an astronaut.

countdown: the counting backwards of time before a launching rocket takes off.

crater: a hole made when a rocky lump from outer space hits the surface of a planet or moon.

D

docking: the joining together of two spacecraft in space.

E

eclipse: the movement of one heavenly body across the face of another. An eclipse of the Sun takes place when the Moon moves across the face of the Sun and blots out its light.

encounter: the time when a spacecraft meets its target in space.

equinox: a time of the year when the lengths of the daytime and night-time are equal. This happens twice a year on about March 21 (spring equinox) and September 23 (autumn equinox).

ESA: the European Space Agency, the body that organizes space activities in Europe.

escape velocity: the speed at which a body must be launched from the Earth to escape from gravity – 40,000 km/h.

EVA: extravehicular activity, or activity outside a spacecraft. The popular term for it is spacewalking.

evening star: the planet Venus shining brightly in the western sky after sunset.

extraterrestrial (ET): outside the Earth; or a being that comes from another world.

F

free fall: the state that exists in orbit where spacecraft travel round and round the Earth. They – and everything inside them – are falling towards the Earth. But the amount they fall equals the amount the Earth's surface curves away beneath them. And so they remain the same distance above the Earth, in orbit.

G

galaxy: a great star 'island' in space. All stars in the Universe gather together in galaxies.

gantry: the structure on a launch pad, from which engineers work on a launching rocket.

geostationary orbit: an orbit around the Equator in which a satellite takes just 24 hours to circle the Earth. It appears to be stationary (fixed) in the sky. The orbit is 35,900 km high.

g-forces: forces set up when a launching rocket speeds away from the launch pad. They make astronauts feel much heavier than they really are.

gravity: the pull of the Earth on everything on it or near it in space. Every heavenly body has a similar pull. The bigger the body, the stronger is the gravity, or gravitational pull.

greenhouse effect: what happens when the atmosphere of a planet traps heat, like a greenhouse does. It causes the planet to heat up. This has happened on Venus, and is starting to happen on Earth.

gravity-assist: using the gravitational pull of a planet to increase the speed of a space probe.

H

heat shield: a layer of material on the outside of a spacecraft, which protects it from heat during re-entry. The heat is produced by friction with the air when the craft re-enters the atmosphere at high speed.

heavens: 'the heavens' is another term for the night sky. Heavenly bodies are the objects we see in the night sky, such as stars, planets, comets and meteors.

hydrogen: the most plentiful substance in the Universe. It is the 'fuel' stars use to produce the energy to shine.

I

interplanetary: between the planets.

interstellar: between the stars.

life-support system: the system in a spacecraft that keeps the human crew alive in space.

light-year: the distance light travels in a year, nearly 10 million million kilometres. Astronomers use the light-year as a unit to measure the distance to the stars.

lunar: to do with the Moon.

M

magnetism: a property possessed by the Earth, some planets, the Sun and the stars. Magnetism sets up invisible forces that attract (pull) and repel (push). We can explore these forces by experimenting with magnets. It is the Earth's magnetism that makes the needle of a compass move.

mare (plural maria): a 'sea', or plain, on the Moon.

meteor: a fiery streak in the night sky, produced when a meteoroid burns up in the Earth's upper atmosphere.

meteorite: a piece of rock from outer space that does not burn up in the atmosphere like a meteor, but hits the ground.

meteoroid: a bit of rocky matter that travels through space.

Milky Way: the fuzzy white band of light that arcs across the heavens. It is also the name of our Galaxy, to which the Sun and the stars in the sky belong.

mission: a space flight.

moon: another term for satellite.

morning star: the planet Venus shining brightly in the eastern sky before sunrise.

N

NASA: the National Aeronautics and Space Administration; the body that organizes space activities in the United States.

nebula: a bright or dark 'cloud' of gas and dust among the stars.

neutron star: a very small and very dense star made up of atomic particles called neutrons.

nova: a star that suddenly becomes very much brighter.

nuclear energy: energy given out during reactions involving the nuclei (centres) of certain atoms. Nuclear reactions involving hydrogen atoms produce the energy that makes the stars shine.

O

orbit: the path taken when one body circles around another in space.

orbital velocity: the speed a satellite needs to remain in orbit around the Earth. It varies with height above the Earth. The orbital velocity at a height of 300 km is about 28,000 km/h.

orbiter: the winged spaceplane that is the main part of the space shuttle system.

P

payload: the 'cargo' a launching rocket carries.

phases: the changes in appearance of the Moon during the month, as we see more or less of it lit up by the Sun.

planet: a large body that orbits around the Sun. The Earth is one of nine planets.

Pole star: a star almost directly above the Earth's North Pole. Its position in the night sky hardly changes at all as the Earth rotates. It is also called the North Star and Polaris.

probe: a spacecraft that escapes from the Earth and travels far into space to explore the planets and other bodies.

propellant: a substance that propels a rocket. It is burned to produce a stream of hot gases.

pulsar: a star that gives off powerful pulses of radio waves and other radiation. Astronomers think it is a rapidly spinning neutron star.

Q

quasar: a quasi-stellar object; a mysterious body that looks like a star but is very much farther away. It is very much smaller than a galaxy, but is brighter than hundreds of galaxies put together.

R

radio astronomy: a branch of astronomy that studies the radio waves coming from objects in space.

red giant: a large red star up to about 100 times bigger across than the Sun. One day the Sun will expand to become a red giant.

re-entry: the moment that a spacecraft re-enters the air when returning to Earth after a space flight.

reflector: a telescope that uses mirrors to gather and focus starlight.

refractor: a telescope that uses lenses to gather and focus starlight.

rocket: an engine that is propelled by a stream of gases escaping from the rear at high speed.

S

satellite: a small body that circles around a larger one in space. Most planets have natural satellites; the Earth has one natural satellite (the Moon) and also many man-made satellites.

seasons: the regular changes in the weather over the year that occur in most places on Earth. They happen because the Earth is tilted on its axis in space as it circles around the Sun every year.

solar: to do with the Sun.

solar cell: an electric cell that turns the energy in sunlight into electricity.

Solar System: the family of the Sun, which includes the planets and their moons, asteroids, meteoroids and comets.

solar wind: a stream of atomic particles given off by the Sun.

solstice: a time of the year when the Sun appears highest or lowest in the sky at noon. In the Northern Hemisphere the Sun reaches its highest point on about June 21 (the summer solstice), and its lowest on about December 21 (the winter solstice).

space: the great emptiness through which the planets, Sun, stars and galaxies travel.

spacesuit: a garment astronauts wear when they go spacewalking, which gives them oxygen to breathe and protects them from the hazards of space.

spacewalking: moving about outside a spacecraft. The activity is properly termed EVA, or extravehicular activity.

star: a great globe of hot gas, which gives out energy as light, heat and other forms of radiation.

stellar: to do with the stars.

step rocket: a combination of rockets, used to form a launching rocket. The separate rocket units (stages) are usually joined end to end.

supergiant: a huge bright star, hundreds of times bigger across than the Sun.

supernova: a supergiant star that blasts itself apart, increasing in brightness millions of times.

T

telescope: the main instrument astronomers use to study the stars. It gathers faint starlight and produces a brighter, magnified image.

terrestrial: to do with the Earth.

tides: the daily rise and fall of the oceans. They are caused by the gravitational pull of the Moon circling around the Earth.

tracking: following a spacecraft travelling through space.

U

UFO: unidentified flying object; a mysterious object seen in the sky, which no one can explain. Some people believe that UFOs come from another world.

Universe: everything that exists: the Earth, the planets, the Sun, the stars and space.

W

weightlessness: the strange state that exists in orbit, where nothing appears to have any weight. The correct term for it is free fall.

white dwarf: a small star that is very dense. The Sun will one day turn into a white dwarf.

INDEX

Note: page numbers printed in **bold type** indicate major references to the topic.

ACKNOWLEDGEMENTS

Quarto would like to thank the following for providing photographs, and for granting permission to reproduce copyright material. We would especially like to thank Spacecharts Photo Library for supplying the majority of these photographs:

Anglo-Australian Telescope Board: 71tr,tl; Astrofotos: 24b, 46c, 48, 49, 50, 54t, 59, 65, 75t; Bell Laboratories: 76b; Heather Angel, Biofotos: 22t & b, 23tl, 23bl & br; Nick Buzzard: 20cl, 21cr; CERN: 76t; Moira Clinch: 13br; E.T. Archive: 15cr, 45cl, 56bl, 62bl; European Space Agency: 47t, 51b, 82t; Geoscience Features: 21b; Eric & David Hosking: 23cl; Robin Kerrod: 61, 31(box), 52t, 54b, 55, 78b, 79b, 80t, 81b, 85tl, 86bl; Kitt Peak National Observatory: 7t, 60, 61, 64, 66, 67, 68, 73b; Courtesy of the London Planetarium: 52br; Bruce Low: 13cr; Mansell Collection: 11cl, 25bc; Mt Wilson Observatory: 78t; NASA: 6r, 7c, 7b, 14, 15, 17, 18t, 19, 24t, 26–30, 31b, 32–40, 41b, 42–44, 45tb, 46t, 46b, 70, 74, 75b, 82, 84, 85tr, 85b, 86t, 86bc, 87–91; National Radio Astronomy Observatories: 41t, 81t; Palomar Observatory: 58, 72; Remote Sensing Unit, RAE Farnborough: 83b; Roque de los Muchachos Observatory: 79t, 80b; Royal Observatory Edinburgh/Anglo-Australian Telescope Board: 51c; TASS: 18b, 86br; TRIP: Helen Rogers 12tr; US Geological Survey: 6c; US Naval Observatory: 71b, 73t; Yerkes Observatory: 48cl.

(b = bottom, c = centre, l = left, r = right, t = top)

Whilst every effort has been made to trace and acknowledge all copyright holders, we would like to apologise should any omissions have been made.